CHECKMATE.

Lorenzo L. Sellers

Success Expert

CHECKMATE

EDITED AND TYPESET BY LORENZO SELLERS

Cover design by Lorenzo Sellers

Printed in the U.S.A.

To order this title, please visit www.createspace.com to order using VISA or MasterCard, or for further information on books from the Sellers Success Group.

The Sellers Success Group, Inc.

5357 Bellefield Rd

Norfolk, VA 23502

"Dedicated to those who are looking for a
way to make it through the storm"

ACKNOWLEDGEMENTS

I honestly would like to thank everyone who has ever believed in me and the dream that I hold to help millions of families become financially free by using the special gifts and talents that they hold. Through the power of love and support, I was able to work up the courage to speak to thousands of people per year, spreading my philosophy of COSA (The Cycle of Successful Achievement). I would also like to thank all my mentors who truly made a difference in my life by teaching me the basic fundamentals to achieving all my dreams.

It was the words of one of my most cherished and most admired mentors that spurred me on. She told to me that, "If I wasn't willing to do whatever it takes to get what I want, I had no right to ask for it and no chance of ever receiving it." Day by day, these words give me strength to keep moving forward despite all the road blocks I come across.

I acknowledge all my fans out there who follow me on my blog weekly to develop themselves and grow into the ultimate them. This book is truly for you.

Lorenzo L Sellers

Lorenzo L Sellers, 2015

Success Expert

CONTENTS

PREFACE

It would seem as though there are A LOT of books out there that promise results in a short amount of time. But seriously, how many of them actually deliver what it promises? During my travels to different countries and seeing different ways of life, one thing remained the same; everybody wants to live a life of freedom. So I decided to find someone who knew how to obtain that way of life. From then to now, I have been studying under the wing of my millionaire mentor, learning her ways of doing business and living life. Based off of what I learned, I wrote a book back in

2013 entitled Achiever, which had a taste of what she taught me.

That book did pretty well considering I was still a new face in the industry of self-improvement and lifestyle development. So I decided to reach a little deeper and create a philosophy that would provide the results necessary that would create real time change. No fluff and definitely no nonsense. The COSA Effect was born. Which stands for "Cycle of Successful Achievement". This philosophy held the three basic but effective tools needed to create a shift in circumstances that would create desired results, no matter what a person's goal may be. I incorporated the COSA into my 2nd book, Million Dollar Mind.

Which was released in December 2013. I later decided that I should release the entire process for the public to see. So in January 2014, The Blueprint to Success was published. Which kicked off my speaking business and had me performing more than 500 talks to more than 5,000 people. After hearing my talks, people would ask me more specific questions like, "How can I apply the COSA to my job?" This forced me to think on a more direct approach toward helping people reach their lofty goals. I asked myself,

Checkmate

"How can I help those who aren't quite ready to venture out on their own and start a business?" A million answers came to me, but one overshadowed them all. Take them on the same journey I undertook within my first year of starting to apply the COSA to my life. But not the broad idea of my philosophy, but a more specific guide if you will.

Now you have the product of what my final idea was in your hands. *Checkmate* will help you to set yourself up for success and become a superstar in the eyes of your employer and clients. It is the key to how I obtained the knowledge to create multiple streams of income other than my job and completely send you on a direct course to seeing massive results in the following year. With every great thing, it takes time. It takes far less time to build a chicken coop than it does to build a skyscraper. So this process will take more than a couple of months to see results. I received many skeptical comments when I announced that I was writing this book.

However, skepticism will keep you broke if you use it and take money out of your pocket if you buy it from someone else. I continued to write what I believe to be one of my best master tools that will change the lives of millions. I've been told to keep the information that is in this book a secret in order to gain the upper hand on the opposition. But I believed that information such as this should be shared so that everyone may taste the flavor of victory.

What you're about to read will revolutionize everything you ever believed and was ever taught to believe. This book is the key to your everlasting success in your business, career, or even your job. It's one thing to earn a degree. But not knowing how to use your own personal power to use your acquired knowledge will render all those years of schooling useless.

You will not be the same person who picked this book up once you finish it. You will be enlightened to the truth behind life and how to acquire wealth beyond your wildest dreams. So if you're ready, let's begin.

INTRODUCTION

The First Year

It is a fact that most famous people you see and know today started off very small. It is a natural way of life that all great things have small beginnings. You're just seeing the tip of the iceberg when you see popular and successful people living the life of luxury. However, very few realize what those individuals had to go through to get where they are now. They all started off just like any normal person. Who they are now is completely different than who they were a year or two ago. Think about it. We live in a society today that wants everything now rather than later.

Checkmate

The lessons that were taught about how to become successful by setting up a proper foundation have been lost and scattered into the winds. You have videos on YouTube that teach these same principles viewed far less than videos that promote unsuccessful habits. I mean seriously, these helpful videos would only have 5,000 views while a video of street fights, twerking, and men dressing as women would have well over 1 million views! Society has lost its way with the times of increasing technology and has gotten quite lazy.

There are advertisements everywhere that promote quick wealth and abundance by giving up thousands of dollars to obtain. All this is making it hard to see past the distractions and reaching the one truth behind success: Obtain the mindset necessary to create the proper plan in line with your goals and act on them. Which is why I created the Cycle of Successful Achievement philosophy.

It has been proven many times that the quicker you gain wealth, the faster you'll lose it if you're not ready to receive it. Take lottery winners for example. How many people do you know who won the lottery for an upwards amount of $200 million dollars taking them out of poverty and who are either on their way or back to poverty?

Those particular individuals weren't ready for wealth because they didn't spend the time required to gain the mindset to hold on to wealth. Anything built on a weak foundation will fall. This falls true when it comes to building a successful career and business. The point to reaching a goal is the experience you gain while on the journey. This is what the first year to building your successful career, business, or the reputation at your job is all about. This is a crucial step for your success.

People just don't become successful in the same year they start working on a dream. What this book has in store for you is what you need to know and do the year prior to see massive results the following year. This book will be a real momentum builder for anyone who would like to see more zeroes in their paycheck. Face the truth now and you will be one step ahead of most people today. If you have been wasting your time cruising through YouTube looking for "waste of time" videos, here is your chance now to come to a decision that will change the foundation of your life.

Checkmate

The fact of the matter is this: If you don't build upon yourself and do what it takes within the first year, you won't see any improvement in the second. The second year will look a whole lot like the first one. People like Steve Harvey, Oprah Winfrey, Bill Gates, and Warren Buffet all started making the necessary moves in their first year that changed the rest of their lives. It's easy to think that these people would have lead very different lives if they never did what they did in the beginning to get to where they are now.

To live a very comfortable life, one must own up and take responsibility over their own actions. Without doing this, there is no way you can control your circumstances. Take the wheel of your life and guide yourself. There is power in becoming a focused individual. Which I will explain later on in this book. The point in taking 1 year to set yourself up is to build momentum. Allow me to explain the effects of using a profound law that works every single time you embrace it's power.

Last year around this time, I learned a very important lesson when it comes to accomplishing the "impossible". Many times, people have started something they were passionate about in the beginning and then stopped when a challenge that seemed "too great" to overcome appeared. We tend to get that, "I'll slow down for now" mentality, and wind up slowing down to a complete stop. I know from personal experience that once you stop, it's really difficult to start again. Especially when it comes to creating a way to generate income, changing your health standards, and starting a new habit.

However, you have people out there who faced their giant, beat the odds, and then proceeded to succeed in a MASSIVE way. How did they do it? How do you overcome the odds and get what you want anyway? Most people would call it "luck". But we should know by now that luck is nothing more than preparedness meeting the moment of opportunity.

So what is it? Pay close attention to the master key to success I am about to unveil to you and the wisdom of this profound law. The key to using the first year to jump start results lies within the undeniable "Law of Momentum". This law indicates that once you start something and continue to move forward despite of the many obstacles that you will face, you will eventually succeed. This has been the foundation of my success ever since I started changing the lives of many.

The Law of Momentum is like a snowball effect when pushed down a snowy mountain. The snowball gets larger over the time it's rolling down the mountain. What seemed small at first is now large. For Steve Jobs, this was no different. He started Apple in a garage with a couple of friends and associates. Most would say that he would have never succeeded if he had quit after the first "no" he got from calling different investors. There's no denying that those who comprehend this law will see challenges, situations, and even failure as stepping stones for growth and a catalyst toward massive success.

The bottom line is this: Use this law to your advantage. Once you stop because your journey got to "hard", it's likely that you'll have to start over from scratch. Which will make your journey that much longer and that much more difficult. For example: It only took me 4 years to become a millionaire simply because I kept my momentum while it took my competitors 40 years because they stopped every time they came across a road bump.

This law works and is incredibly powerful. Will you take advantage of this law or will you kill your momentum by allowing outside forces such as discouraging talks from friends and family, challenges, situations, and circumstances to dictate your journey? The choice, when it comes down to it, is completely yours. This is the basis behind this book. Building up enough momentum to send your income to new record highs as soon as year two rolls around.

Now the only question left is this: What is it that you need to do to build such massive momentum? Throughout the rest of this book, you will learn, step by step, what it is that you need to do to place yourself in an unprecedented spot for next year. It's going to take time. However, I can guarantee you that if you use every single month maximizing what you're about to learn, you will see the results I promised to you.

Principle 1

The Power of Your Mind

Did you know that the most powerful tool you have is your mind? By thinking alone, you're generating the power needed to completely change your life around. The more time you spend on a singular thought, no matter if it's negative or positive, the more it reflects in your actions. We as human beings live our lives based off of the chain of thoughts we concentrate on. When you dwell on the thought of your last break up, your actions will reflect whatever feeling is generated from that experience. When you think on a plan that will take you to a new level of income, you begin to incorporate actions dedicated to that thought.

Checkmate

Your mind is truly powerful and can be used to create answers to our most challenging problems. However, why is it that so many people fail to use their minds properly by not thinking of solutions to their problems? Most of the time, people tend to spend so much time worrying about things that won't happen instead of creating their futures using the gift of thought. No one is without problems. It is all a part of living. But let me show you how much time we waste in worrying about the wrong problems. Here is a reliable estimate of what people worry about most of the time:

- Things that will never happen: **40%**
- Past things that can't be changed by worrying: **30%**
- Needless health worries: **12%**
- Petty, miscellaneous worries: **10%**
- Real, legitimate worries: **8%**

There are two kinds of problems that we face: the kind that can be solved by us and the kind that is beyond our ability to solve. Most problems fall into the ones that can be solved by us. So we dedicate massive amount of time worrying, when we should be using our powerful minds to come up with solutions. The reason I'm digging into the subject of worrying is because this plays a huge role in your workplace or business.

Checkmate

You will or already have faced numerous problems that will force you to worry more and think less. It's best that you embrace the fact that no matter where you go and what you do in life, you will always bump into problems. One thing you must learn about life is that you could be doing either or. You could waste time by worrying about the effects of that problem that came up at work or you can utilize your time toward solving that problem which will make you the hero. This is what makes the difference between an expendable and a superstar.

Another ability that your mind is capable of is self-creation. You become what you think about! I never thought that I would be speaking to millions of people per year. The only thing I had to do was visualize myself doing such a task. I started to talk like a speaker, think like a philosopher, and write like a bestselling author. The benefits behind me using the power of self-creation was astronomical! My hunger for knowledge on the subject of success grew day by day. The more people I helped, the more I wanted to learn about life to become a better coach.

There is great power behind the person who can use his mind to create his reality. If you see yourself as the manager, commit to the thought, and act on it, you will find yourself going the extra mile every day. You will eventually find yourself in the position of manager. The same goes for becoming the CEO and creating your very own multi-million dollar business.

Which brings us to using the source of all creativity and the final point on the power of your mind. For centuries, people have been searching for the source of ideas that can transform a person's life financially forever. Few people figured out what it took. It is the source of our creativity. It's where crazy ideas come from and how one's bank account jumps up several zeroes. Allow me to reveal to you a concept that will change your entire way of thinking when it comes to being the originator of great ideas.

If you want to increase what is in your real world bank account, draw from your "IBA" (Infinite Bank Account). Rather than money being in this inner account, are ideas and concepts worth millions. All you have to do to withdraw from this account and cash in on those ideas is to act on them. Simple to do for the few who understands this basic concept. They are the people who other people are working for. For many who understands this concept and choose to go for the "illusion of being safe" route, this may be a hard and rather difficult concept to grasp.

However, the key to having a massive bank account is to have a very open mind. Those who find it hard to commit to this concept are the very same people who commit their time, money, and resources to build millions for other people.

People like Bill Gates used this very same concept when he created Microsoft. Mark Zuckerberg also withdraw from his IBA to create Facebook making him the youngest billionaire ever. We all have an IBA within our minds. The question is: How do you access this vault of gold?

-   Find a quiet place to go to. No distractions. No TV, no computer, no radio. All you should have with you is a pen and paper to write down your ideas

-   Close your eyes and reach back into the darkest regions of your mind.

- Think back to when you had an "ah ha" moment or when a crazy idea hit you.

- Think of things you see that can be done better if done differently, no matter how silly you think it is. Make sure it's something that you feel confident that you can accomplish if you set your mind to it. If you feel you can't, do it anyway and surprise yourself.

- Open your eyes and write down all the ideas and new concepts that you withdraw from your IBA.

In the most common case, this is critical thinking. However, looking at it from the perspective of withdrawing from an inner bank account will help many to overcome the thought of this being a hard task. Take some time to go over this principle and make as many withdrawals as you wish. There is no limit to what you can accomplish and no limit to your abundant ideas.

Also when using your mind, you must learn that without expansion, there is no growth. You know what you know and can only perform up to what knowledge you have already acquired. Remember that whatever goes on within the darkest regions of your mind will surely reflect on your outside actions. What does this mean for you and your income?

What you think about and how you think about them will determine the level of income you earn, the type of house you live in, the type of car you drive, the type of relationships you have, etc. Take a look at what you have right now. Everything that you have around you will tell you what type of thoughts you grant attention to.

This can make a real impact on your life. Since your most dominate thoughts will determine the type of actions you take which will determine the type of lifestyle you live, it would be best to expand your mind by learning all that you can. A person who only knows of working for wages cannot hope to attain the millionaire mark. But by learning and applying different and honorable ways to earn income, the chances of attaining such a mark increase. I know we all said it before, "we heard that before. It's nothing new". There is a reason why so many people still work for wages and a small amount earn giant amounts of income. Because one may have heard helpful information before, doesn't mean that one utilizes it.

It is not enough to just "know" about something. It's useless if you don't put it to practical use. Here is one secret to success: Listen from those who have gone to where you want to go (i.e. books, mentors, programs, seminars), apply those steps to your own venture, and leave nature no choice but to send success your way.

This alone will change the way you think. Therefore, changing your actions and creating a different set of results you wouldn't have gotten if you didn't apply the one secret to success. This also works on other aspects other than money. The bottom line: Expand your mind in the direction you want to go, exceed your limits, and create desired results. Remember the power that you hold in your mind.

Principle 2

One Who Good Fortune Favors

How many times have you seen someone that you may or may not know, always receive what they want? Those very few are often times called the "lucky ones" or the "blessed". It doesn't seem to matter what the circumstances are for them. If they want something, they'll get it. And the speed in which they get their prize is so great, one would think that they made a deal with the devil himself.

However, the key to receiving such a gift of good fortune lies dormant in those who have yet to recognize the full potential that they have. There are two types of people in the world that both hold the power. Except one of those types control the positive end of that power. Just like everything else in this world, there are two sides to fortune. One side gives you everything you want and need; the other side gives you less desirable results. What side you wind up using depends on the type of person you are.

The first type of person are those who have no aims in life. They have no goals set and absolutely no plans to follow. They are the ones who make up the greatest number of "employees" in big name companies, small stores, and warehouses. They are the followers to those who created the master plan by setting a goal and acting on it. They are the ones who would rather blame others for their mistakes and refuse to take responsibility. They are the ones who would rather watch television all day instead of using that time to develop themselves. They are the individuals who work on many projects, but finish none.

This particular type of person goes with the flow and allows life to happen to them while waiting patiently on a miracle to solve all their problems. 98% of the world's population today falls into the category of the "distracted". There is no way possible for anyone who chooses to stay in the whirlpool of the distracted to obtain their most wanted desires in this world. Those who aspire to nothing will gain just that, nothing. You would find one of the distracted wallowing in their own dark corner of self-pity. This kind constantly complains about how unfair life is. Let's not forget the sense of entitlement that takes up most of the distracted belief system.

This is by far the most dangerous aspect of the distracted. The mind is never without some type of thought unless the person is brain dead. With thoughts of entitlement taking up your mind, there will be little to no increase in your annual income. Your career, business, or job will go absolutely nowhere. Without progression, there is only death that awaits you. Death of your career, death of your business, and unemployment will all become a thing of reality.

By allowing thoughts other than becoming successful to take over a great percentage of your mind, you're allowing the devil to do his handy work on you. Every negative thought that you allow to grow, you can bet that your circumstances won't get better, situations will spiral out of control, and your boss (*if you have one*) will continue to make your experience in the workplace a living hell. Once not too long ago, I had a client who fell into the category of the distracted. He had so many great ideas that he wanted to work on. So he did, only to find out that nothing was getting done at all. Often times, the few that actually do act on their dream of becoming financially free fall short by starting on a million things all at the same time.

I advised him to do what the other type of person that I am about to reveal to you would do. To focus on one major project at a time. By finishing one project that is generating income, you can now begin another. The type of person that life grants good fortune to is called the "focused". Those who focus on what they want tend to get just that. They are the ones who are always developing themselves. They are the leaders of major companies. They are the ones who set goals and act on them.

They are the ones who seem to always get that raise at work. They are the ones who live on the best street, driving the newest car, and always wearing the best clothes. They are the ones who are always smiling and sharing ideas with the rest of the world. They are courageous and never allow fear to keep them in one spot. It goes back to that saying, "Life favors the bold". That was half the secret. What it should say is that: "Life favors the focused". If you truly think about it, great men and women who have done great and even terrible things to and for this world falls into this category of people. No matter if your goal is good or evil, by staying focused on your target, you will hit it.

Oprah Winfrey's story provides proof of my claims. In 1994, with talk shows becoming increasingly trashy and exploitative, Winfrey pledged to keep her show free of tabloid topics. Although ratings initially fell, she earned the respect of her viewers and was soon rewarded with an upsurge in popularity. Her projects with Harpo have included the highly rated 1989 TV miniseries, The Women of Brewster Place, which she also starred in. Winfrey also signed a multi-picture contract with Disney. The initial project, 1998's Beloved, based on Pulitzer Prize-winning novel by Toni Morrison and starring Winfrey and Danny Glover, got mixed reviews and generally failed to live up to expectations.

Winfrey, who became almost as well-known for her weight loss efforts as for her talk show, lost an estimated 90 pounds (dropping to her ideal weight of around 150

Checkmate

pounds) and competed in the Marine Corps Marathon in Washington, D.C., in 1995. In the wake of her highly publicized success, Winfrey's personal chef, Rosie Daley, and trainer, Bob Greene, both published best-selling books.

The media giant contributed immensely to the publishing world by launching her "Oprah's Book Club," as part of her talk show. The program propelled many unknown authors to the top of the bestseller lists and gave pleasure reading a new kind of popular prominence.

With the debut in 1999 of Oxygen Media, a company she co-founded that is dedicated to producing cable and Internet programming for women, Winfrey ensured her place in the forefront of the media industry and as one of the most powerful and wealthy people in show business. In 2002, she concluded a deal with the network to air a prime-time complement to her syndicated talk show.

Her highly successful monthly, O: The Oprah Magazine debuted in 2000, and in 2004, she signed a new contract to continue The Oprah Winfrey Show through the 2010-11 season. Now syndicated, the show is seen on nearly 212 U.S. stations and in more than 100 countries worldwide making her the first self-made African American billionaire in the United States.

She is a prime example of what one of the focused is capable of doing. By sticking to what you believe in, acting on your goals, and staying focused on your goals, you will reach them and life will yield to you everything that you could ever want and need. No matter how meager your job may be right now, no matter if your career is dangerously close to coming to an end, or your business is slowly fading, by performing the right actions that I am going to show you throughout this book, you can and will save your own life. You too can become just as successful as Oprah.

Embrace the lifestyle of the focused and everything else will fall into place. We all live in a world that provides for those who are determined to reach their goals and are willing to do what it takes to achieve them. Makes you wonder why only 2% of the population (the percentage that controls 98% of the money flow) utilizes this ageless truth. Why would most of the population choose to be distracted, knowing that life is meaningless without some sort of goal? Most fear success because it may be an unknown entity to them. Others fear the possibility of failure, therefore never starting because of it.

People tend to fear what they do not understand and what they cannot see right away. In today's world, if results cannot be seen right away, no one is interested in being focused. So they rather be distracted by things that cannot possibly yield results of any kind. So let's end this chapter with five main points you should take away with you:

Seeds of Greatness:

- ♟ Life favors the "FOCUSED"
- ♟ In this life, you will either be FOCUSED or DISTRACTED.
- ♟ Life will give you whatever you set your sights and mind on; negative or positive
- ♟ Wealth of all kinds are attracted to those who focus on ONE project and completes that project before they start on another.
- ♟ God's gift is the power of FOCUS. The devil's gift is that of DISTRACTION.

Principle 3

The Billion Dollar Thought

"It doesn't matter what you encounter on the road ahead; what does matter is the light that you shed on those encounters." These were that last words I spoke to one of my clients at the end of our contract. Within the last phase of my coaching program, I share the "Billion Dollar Thought" with all my clients. This is a certain way of thinking that will propel you to higher levels of achievement within your business, career, or job.

Although a very simple concept, it has been proven that many people struggle with this step in my program. Our thoughts carry a significant role in how we respond to different situations and challenges that we endure in our lives. With that being said, it is important that we realize the power that we hold in controlling most of our circumstances in life. Yes, you did read that correctly. You hold the power to controlling 98.5% of your situations and circumstances.

I remember a time when I was in a restaurant and asked the workers there how they viewed "problems". One of the workers said that they saw problems as obstacles they eventually have to overcome. The other one said that problems vary from person to person. They were both right in the general sense. But then I shared the Billion Dollar Thought with them that would soon change the way they lived life. I responded with this:

"I want you both to remember this and use this in your everyday thinking. Your problems are the manifestation of all your worries of an outcome that will never happen. The key to eliminating all your problems is to stop worrying. Then your problems become challenges that you can and will easily overcome eventually."

At that moment, they both had an "ah ha" expression on their faces. Similar to the one that you could be making right now. The reason why this is called the "Billion Dollar Thought" lies in the fact that this way of thinking will shrink all your "problems" into small road bumps. Everybody has their own challenges to deal with. But what may seem like a problem to you, may not be a problem to your business associates. It's all about how you view those "problems" that you're encountering.

I had to come to this truth myself years ago when I first arrived in San Diego, California. I transferred to a different command coming from Washington State. Bills began to stack high, debts were getting deeper, and my stress was rising to even greater heights due to the inflation of the cost of living. I was a mess to say the least. I allowed, what seemed at the time as problems, to become a burden on me and my pockets. The moment that changed my life and the path I was taking forever happened one night when I spoke to my "inner counsel" through my dreams. For those of you who don't know what an inner counsel is, you can refer to Napoleon Hill's "Think and Grow Rich" for the answer.

The answer I got back was astounding! By looking at my problems in a different light, they became easier to manage. I no longer allowed those challenges to stress me out. If anything, I began to have fun overcoming these obstacles. Isn't it amazing how a simple turn in thought can completely change the rules of the game? I began to see how all those millionaires and billionaires got to where they are today.

We all face our problems differently. But how we choose to view those problems will determine if we step down and land in deeper water, hesitate to move at all and continue to allow the problem to exist, or to view the problem as a challenge and step up to grow to a level where the problem is easy to solve. Throughout your journey, you will face obstacles designed to stump you. The lesson here is to view those obstacles as stepping stones to a greater purpose. A simple change in the direction of the tide can take you to a different destination.

Here are six practical tips for overcoming your challenges:

Don't See Your Challenge As A Problem:

The first thing that comes to the mind of most people with challenges is that they begin to see their challenges as limitations to their success.

The moment you begin to see your challenges as "problems", you start to have more "problems" because worry and fears begin to set in. The truth is, the way you see your challenges determines how they will affect you.

If you see your challenges as the walls of Jericho (that cannot be broken down) rather than opportunities in disguise, then those challenges will affect you more than they are supposed to. But if you see your challenges as opportunities in disguise then you will be able to tackle them and get the message that the "problems" are trying to pass across to you.

Remain Positive:

The greatest of men are known to always remain calm when they face their challenges. They are used to speaking positively so when they face challenges, they still remain positive.

Staying positive is one of the keys to solving your problems and when used well could help get you out of difficulties. When you remain positive, you put yourself in the right position to tackle your problems effectively.

Learn From The Challenge:

There is no problem in this world that does not come with something new to learn from it and with every lesson comes a tangible solution.

You must understand that it is not all about being positive and not seeing the challenge as a problem alone, but also about learning from the challenge itself and looking for the way forward rather than complaining, worrying and giving excuses.

Every challenge you face is just like an examination and once you pass the obstacle standing in your way, you get elevated to the next level. Before every examination is a lesson that brings positive answers to the question set in the examination. The challenge that did not kill you has just added to you, made you stronger, given you a new experience and has just tested you to know if you're fit for the next position God is taking you to.

Remain Focused And Determined:

There is no battle that can be won in life without remaining focused and determined and like my millionaire mentor would always tell me: *"determination is the key to great achievements"*.

Many people have learned from their challenges and they know what would get them out of this obstacle, but they are not determined and focused enough.

Have Someone You Can Always Speak With:

Not everybody is fit to undertake your challenges with you, and not everybody is fit to know the obstacles set in front of you. But it's advisable to have someone you can speak to, that could serve as an advisor and a mentor to you, someone that can monitor your progress and someone that is trustworthy and would always be willing to listen to you. Just as I do for my clients.

You must be able to be accountable to this person and the person must be someone that is better and more knowledgeable than you. This person would be able to give you meaningful advice, monitor your progress and also support you in prayers.

Remember That God Is Able:

There are three kinds of people I know: those that remember God only when they have troubles, those that forget God when they have troubles and those that always serve God whether there is trouble or not. The wise people fall into the third category.

Here we are at the end of this chapter and some things you should take away from it.

Seeds of Greatness:

- Problems are the manifestation of all your worries of an outcome that will never happen.

- Problems won't exist once you stop worrying. Put your faith in God and act on them as though you cannot fail.

- Challenges arise. Accept it as a part of your journey toward success.

Principle 4

You, Inc.

Envision this if you will: Today is the day before you start that new job you finally landed. A million thoughts are racing through your head as to what mindset you should have when you first walk into the workplace. This is a critical moment for anyone's first day. We already went over what the first year is all about, the power that you hold within your mind, what brings good fortune, and the thought that creates billionaires. Now you will learn what point of view takes a person from janitor to CEO.

Checkmate

With any job that requires you to be an employee, there will always be a boss. There is another human being that has complete ownership over your time. However, it doesn't have to be this way for you. Once you fall into the "employee mindset", the control of your time, resources, and even your money belongs to your boss. Is this truly what you want? If you picked up this book, I'm guessing that you're looking for another route that will take you toward financial freedom. Because having the "employee mindset" definitely won't get you there.

This is when you must take back control of your own time and realize the true nature of your services. Here is the no nonsense truth:

"You work for nobody else but yourself"

Employers will never tell you this. Allow me to explain to you why this is so. It takes the mental control away from them and places it back into your capable hands. Think about it this way. You wake up every day to go to work in order to earn money to keep your lights on, to put food on the table, to pay off that car note you may have, and to be able to afford things that you want once all your needs are taken care of. And the level of income you earn annually is completely up to you once you adapt to the "You, Inc. mindset".

You're providing your services to the employer. Now the question is: What is your mission when you go into work? The great majority of people go to work simply to earn a paycheck by doing the bare minimum. This is when the Law of Equal Exchange comes into play. You get back in pay exactly what you give out. Bare minimum work equals to bare minimum pay and not a cent more. This is the employee mindset. Look at yourself as a consulting business that is offering a service to another business. You are your own corporate giant!

This is why it's so important that you realize what you can really offer. Hone in on your skills by raising your value to the marketplace. It was the great Jim Rohn that once said, *"Work harder on yourself than you do on your job."* Once you become valuable to that business you're providing your services to, your pay begins to increase almost immediately. This is when you begin to climb that ladder. You will be rewarded with higher positions of pay and more responsibilities. This isn't for the mass majority of people. It has been proven many times that a lot of people have yet to take full responsibility of their own lives yet.

So the competition in today's world is very slim. Why reward someone with more responsibility if they haven't grasped the concept of taking ownership of their own lives yet? As once stated, we live in a country where people feel that they are entitled to money. The sense of entitlement will only halt you from earning money. This is the very thing that will keep a person in poverty. If this is you, take some time to destroy this way of thinking immediately before you continue with this book.

The methods that are designed in this book wouldn't work for the person who feels entitled to money. Remember this, the world owes you nothing. To accumulate wealth, one must provide some sort of product or service in exchange for money. Ask yourself this question: "If I were in the customer's and/or employer's shoes, why would I pay high for my services?"

It's a career changing question that very few ask themselves. If your "business" had a five star rating system, how many stars would you receive based on your own efforts? Be completely honest with yourself. Right now, we are building You, Inc. with asking soul searching questions that will help you see where you are right now. After years of studying the marketplace, I have come to realize that value is everything.

I had no idea that the value of your personal services controlled how much you earned annually. The marketplace is brutally honest as well. If you're only earning $20,000 a year, then your services are only worth $1,666 per month. Which is only $833 every two weeks. I only use these numbers as an example. However if you're earning less than $20,000 per year, then it should be quite obvious where you are right now and should be an indicator that your marketplace value is low.

We need to increase your self-business revenue by increasing your value to the employer. Here are a few ways that you can make that possible:

The Power of Relationships

Life is about relationships, and nowhere is that more apparent than the workplace. People hire people, companies don't hire people. It's important that you work hard and are a competent employee, of course, but you also need to be likable and fit in with the corporate culture. You will find that if you have a good relationship with the people who you work with (and for), you will be far more likely to get chosen for leadership roles or to be part of groups within the workplace.

Over Deliver

One of the things that most people take for granted is how easy it is to surprise someone. As an organization, or as an employee, simply doing a tiny bit more than what is expected will go a LONG way in the overall perception of your performance and increasing your value. For example, let's say you were asked to write a blog post for the company website.

If you take an extra half an hour and write a second blog post (it's really not that hard!) the content manager will have a tremendous perception of you. Even if he isn't your direct manager, those things have a way of making their way back to your superiors.

Expand Your Responsibilities

Going along with the concept of over-delivering, it's important to gradually expand your responsibilities whenever you have the opportunity to do so. Perhaps someone leaves the organization, and their role needs to be split up while they search for a replacement. Volunteering to take on some of that additional work will position you as a team player, and may also make you more valuable to the organization, as a better rounded employee.

Become Known as an Expert at Something

This is a very important one to increasing your value. Becoming an expert at something that is important to the organization will make you an invaluable resource. Participate in industry events, write articles for third party publications, do whatever you can to position yourself within your company and your industry. It will make your company, and in turn, you, look very good!

Make Your Boss Look Good

Finally, making your boss look good will do a great deal for your career and adding to your professional value. That is not to say that you need to be a constant brown-nose, but through your work and your growing responsibility, make your boss look like he/she is running a strong team, and is accomplishing a great deal for the company. When a promotion or a raise becomes available, your boss is likely to look more favorably on you. Also, when your boss moves up the ranks, he/she will probably bring you up the chain as well!

I once had a client named Brian who has had trouble rising through the ranks at his current workplace. He was in competition with one other person at the time and at first was having the hardest time shining because his competition worked at the company longer. He found me on the internet and enlisted my help. By applying the self-business mindset, he was able to overcome his challenge and is now the Vice President of the entire company and doing extremely well for himself. Here is his story:

Brian has been working for this corporation for 7 years now. He is constantly early to work and the last to leave at the end of the day. His performance is impeccable and people who he works with really enjoy his presence around the office. Brian's job is really demanding as he handles the financials of the company.

But he also takes on other jobs and tasks in different departments to further his thirst for experience. He always shows up with a smile on his face and a song in his heart. If positivity had a face, it would be Brian's. Evaluations are coming up and this could be the chance he was waiting for to be promoted to the Head Sales Manager that he applied for, but he has competition.

Steve has been working there for 9 years. Steve is also early to work every day and one of the last people to take off at the end of the day. His performance is also impeccable in what he does but his attitude drives people away. Steve complains a lot about his job there and how he believes he is smarter than his employer, therefore, believing that no further improvement of his work is needed. He works in the sales department of the company and he also applied for the same position as Brian.

So as far as sales go, Steve has more experience than Brian does. The CEO and the board of directives look at both the profiles of the two candidates. Who do you think got the promotion? It was a dead lock at first. But they eventually gave the promotion to Brian.

What could have changed the tie into a landslide? Steve had more experience and had seniority over Brian. So why did Brian end up winning the day? The CEO called those who worked with them both and asked who would they suggest to take the position? Because of Brian's uplifting and positive attitude, it motivated other people to do a little more.

He is an inspiration to the office and a valuable asset to the company. One person's good vibes can turn the tide of many. Even though Brian had little to no experience in sales, his service and overall enthusiasm gave him the potential of being very coachable. His mind was open to receive new information and expand.

Remember, in the work setting, it's not always the more experienced that gets the promotion, but the person who can serve with a smile. The road toward becoming the best won't be an easy one, but it will be well worth it. Here are some things you should definitely take away with you from this chapter before you head in to work:

Seeds of Greatness:

- You are your own company that provides services to another business.

- If you want control of how much you earn per year, now is the time to launch You, Inc.

- Raising your value in the marketplace will raise the level of income you earn.

- You work for nobody else but yourself. Represent yourself well.

Principle 5

The "Selfie" System

In today's world, "selfie" is a term used when someone snaps solo photos of themselves. However, in this book, this term has an entirely different meaning behind it. Before you go dominate the world and become massively successful, there is one very important factor that must be "all together". *YOU.* You, my friend, are the piece that completes the puzzle. Just like there is no tree without first being a seed, there can be no success in your life without you first becoming a success on the inside.

Oprah Winfrey coined it best when she said, "there is no real "doing" in the world without first "being". From this point on, the word "selfie" to you is going to be used as a term that reminds you to "start building within yourself" before you can start building anything else on the outside. I remember a story my mentor told me when I first discovered what I wanted to do as my life's work.

There was a father and his boy sitting in their home one warm Sunday morning. The father was reading his paper like he normally does for a couple of hours and his boy was restless. To keep the boy out of his hair while he concentrated on his paper, the boy's father gave him an old puzzle with the picture of the Earth he found in the attic several weeks before. The boy began on the puzzle right away. Relieved, the father sat back down and continued with his paper.

An hour passed and the boy finished the puzzle. The father was amazed that he finished it as quickly as he did. He asked the boy, how on earth did you finish this puzzle so fast? The boy replied, "There was a picture of a man on the back. Once the man was together, the world was too. The father smiled and hugged his son. "That's right son.

Checkmate

When the man is all together, his world is all together."

The lesson to be learned from this story: You're the root to your own success. You're the meat and potatoes. Everything else is the gravy. Which is why this principle is so important and crucial toward your growth throughout the year. While working with one of my clients who was going through a difficult transition from employee to business owner, I found that there was a need for a deeper self-development program for those who were seeking a complete 360° change in their lives.

This is when I implemented The "Selfie" System into my coaching program. This system was designed to tap into the seven different cycles of the human transformation period. By focusing solely on these points, it is entirely possible for anybody to achieve anything that they desire. This system strengthens the foundation of human thought and creates the "fuel" needed to accomplish the "impossible".

Now we will break down these seven cycles into seven simple terms that you can easily commit to memory: *Self-evaluation, Self-Awareness, Self-Commitment, Self-Belief, Self-Approval, Self-Image, and Self-Fulfillment.* Let's begin dissecting the system so you can take full advantage of its benefits.

Self-Evaluation

This is one of the hardest cycles to deal with. During the self-evaluation cycle, you will be asking yourself the questions that will define who you are. To many people, one of the hardest things to do is to be brutally honest with themselves. With this being the first cycle and the most difficult to overcome, the benefits of completing this cycle will result in a total breakthrough to entering into your own universe.

What I mean by this you may ask. Everyone with a job, at some point in time, has been "evaluated" by their "superiors". You may have been told that you need to improve in certain areas of your work. This is all based on what they have seen from your work. How would you like to be ahead of the power curve? Here are a couple of sets of questions that will gauge you on your job.

Checkmate

Self-Evaluation Questions for Your Job

These questions can help you prepare for your performance evaluation. As you read each question, think about your performance, your progress, and your plans for future development and growth.

1.) What critical abilities does my job require? To what extend do I fulfill them?

2.) What do I like best about my job? Least?

3.) What were my specific accomplishments during this appraisal period?

4.) Which standards or goals did I fall short of meeting?

5.) How could my supervisor help me do a better job?

6.) Is there anything that the institution or my supervisor does that hinders my effectiveness?

7.) What changes would improve my performance?

8.) Does my present job make the best use of my capabilities? How could I become more productive?

9.) What do I expect to be doing five years from now?

10.) Do I need more experience or training in any aspect of my current job? How could it be accomplished?

11.) What have I done since my last evaluation to prepare myself for more responsibility?

12.) What new standards and goals should be established for the next evaluation period? Which old ones need to be modified or deleted?

13.) Did my supervisor provide feedback on my work performance throughout the year?

14.) Did I communicate my questions and/or concerns about my work performance with my supervisor during the past year?

By working on these perspective points, you will notice that your performance has improved and your annual salary jumped up by the minimum of 30%. However, let's go a little deeper and access the deeper regions of your being. Remember, that working hard at your job will only take you so far. But working harder on yourself will yield to you the universe itself.

Here are some questions that will get the very best out of you. These were the very same questions I asked myself before I began the journey to self-made wealth. The key here is to be completely honest with yourself when answering. By answering these questions, you may uncover some facts about yourself that you never would have thought were true.

To get the very best out of these, write them down in your own notebook and answer them when you have the time to think a little deeper on each individual question. Remember, the mission here is to find and create a solid foundation for you.

Self-Evaluation For A Better Life

1.) Am I living up to the full potential of my being?

Checkmate

2.) Am I allowing outside circumstances, situations, and people to dictate my standards of living?

3.) What do I truly believe in when it comes to money?

4.) Do I get jealous when I see other people succeed or am I empowered by it?

5.) Am I living out my life by my expectations of it or other people's expectations of it?

6.) Have I taken full responsibility of my life or am I still blaming other circumstances, situations, and people for the actions I take?

7.) What am I doing right now to take hold of the future I want?

8.) Am I taking advice from people who are where I want to be or from people who never left the front porch?

9.) Out of all my friends, how many of them would encourage me to act on and go after my dreams?

10.) Am I truly focused on obtaining what I really want out of life or am I distracted by things that could never help me get to where I want to be?

11.) Have I accepted failure as a part living a successful life? If not, why?

12.) What am I doing right now that is helping me to become better than I was yesterday?

13.) Am I constantly striving to be the best person that I can be?

14.) What am I afraid of?

15.) Am I ready to accept success and everything that comes with it?

Self-evaluation will lead you to self-discovery. The human mind and soul is such a wonderful gift to the world that those who have discovered and utilized "themselves" has changed it by giving us so many blessings such as the automobile, the traffic light, the iPad, a new sense of hope, etc. However, there are a lot of people who wander around this planet their entire lives and still don't know who they truly are and what they are truly capable of.

Checkmate

Why is that? Because one of the hardest things to do is to ask ourselves the hard hitting questions that would expose our deepest fears and what we believe to be our most embarrassing qualities. Here is the secret: *It's not the questions of ourselves that we are willing to answer that will hold the key to true self-discovery, but the questions that we aren't so willing to answer at all.* It's the hard questions that you ask yourself and answer that will unshackle you from the chains of self-doubt and worry.

The effects of evaluating yourself would result in a more powerful existence and a much more abundant lifestyle. I know how it feels to finally ask and answer the questions that I wasn't willing to answer at first. It's the most liberating feeling that you would ever experience. This much I can promise you: if you don't know how it feels to float like a feather, read over the questions I have provided to you, take your answers to heart, and you will see results from every endeavor that you get involved in.

Checkmate

Self-Awareness

This is when we tap into your once dormant power. One of the most powerful things you can ever be in life is to be aware of yourself. It's the one thing that can give you complete control over your thoughts, emotions, and other factors that controls what happens inside your own mind. Too many people go through life taking on challenges and getting into relationships without truly knowing who they are first. It's like promoting a product to a prospect when you know little to nothing about the product yourself.

This is a tremendous level to embrace for your business or your career. It will take your life to a different level entirely. Imagine that you have been wearing a ball and chain on both of your ankles for your entire life. Day by day, you dealt with all of your life's major challenges being weighed down by self-doubt (Ball 1) and uncertainty (Ball 2).

Think about how you've been dealing with all your problems with half to little of your full capacity. Now imagine that you did a self-evaluation on yourself and asked yourself the hard hitting questions to find the keys that would unlock both your weights. To your surprise, you find exactly what you have been searching for. Now you're finally free to do whatever it is that you desire. It's amazing how life opens up to you once you know exactly what you want because you know who you are and what you're capable of.

This is when we reach the major question: Have I taken full inventory of my life? Many people try to get ahead in life without stopping to realize what they already have. Part of being aware of yourself is knowing how far you came from where you used to be. This way of thinking and point of view pays dividends over time. Your productivity would continue to increase because you would continuously evaluate your overall performance. This level was one of the most freeing stages of life I had ever went through.

This is one of the most important levels to break through when you're running a coaching/consulting business. My income didn't shoot upwards until I became fully aware of my gifts and talents as an author and influential speaker. This became very obvious when I finally reached the $100,000 mark from my speaking events and workshops. It's as though you're holding the wheel to the vehicle we all call life. This is more than wishful, wonderful, and whimsical thinking.

The method of self-awareness is very real and very ground breaking. It's the simple and yet important things such as this we tend to miss. Perhaps we miss things like these because we live in a world that mostly promote events and circumstances that provide the perfect distraction from ourselves. I dare you to spend an entire day to yourself without any television, cell phones, or any other distractions that would cloud your focus upon yourself. You will be surprised at the power you'll find.

Self-Commitment

Here we reach a level much needed to carry out any promise you've made, finish any endeavor you started, and to take your career to levels you never thought possible. However, this is also a level that many people tend to struggle with. How many people do you know who just can't seem to follow through with anything? They have enough motivation to start something, but not enough to see it through to the end.

To accomplish anything, especially if you plan on reaping the benefits of the seed you're planting this year, you must be committed to watering and caring for your seed. In this case, you must do what is necessary to ensure that all your smart work pays off in the end. What can cause a person to self-commit to becoming the best in their field of work, the best in the marketplace, or grow their business to the next level?

The magic word here is *passion*. Passion is the essence of commitment. Without having the passion behind what you want to do, it would be rather difficult to stay interested in whatever you would like to pursue. Passion is that which deeply stirs us. It's the fire from within and that which motivates us. When passion is missing, our actions lack meaning and we don't get the results we want. Without passion, our actions are obligatory and lack velocity. Commitment emanates from passion -- passion is the seed from which commitment blossoms!

Checkmate

The grand question here is: Does this place peak my curiosity of income growth potential? If you don't have this answer in mind, finding a new place of employment where your curiosity is peaked is highly recommended. Unless you fully intend to waste your time and, often times, waste your entire life at a place that you have no intention of rising to the top at. Curiosity creates the hunger for growth and provides the persistence needed to potentially raise one's income to great heights.

When I started my journey down the path of becoming a success expert, I was intensely curious about the effects that personal development has had on the world. My hunger for knowledge on the subject grew every day. I've read hundreds of books on the subject, attended seminars, and even spent hours at a time on YouTube watching videos of speakers and other experts talk about it. Even to this day, I still look for answers to the vault of questions I have. And while looking for those answers, without noticing it, my income grew. By applying what I have learned to my business and my life, the

Checkmate

effects of it helped me produce 3 books. One of them being a bestseller.

I didn't tell you these facts to impress you but to impress upon you the effects of being self-committed. Commitment requires two things: Commitment requires insight and self-awareness. One must know what one's values and ideals are in order to commit to them! Do you know someone who's a conscientious and productive worker but who's not happy? Such a person frequently lacks insight and self-awareness. Commitment is difficult if you don't know what's most important to you! It requires an ability to observe self and make conscious decisions.

This is why commitment is purposeful. It truly involves choice. It means saying yes to our values and to our passions! One must realize that commitment is never haphazard or random. While we may lose our perspective from time to time, commitment always involves choice and intent. It enables us to be purposeful. This is why you see so many people, who are achieving their dreams, move as though they already know what they were created for; the primary reason why they were born. Have a purpose in mind and you will create the ingredient that that brings the forth commitment: vision.

Which brings us to this question: Does commitment generate the envisioning process, or does vision generate commitment? Either way, commitment and vision are inexplicably tied together. Expand your vision while you deepen your commitment in order to produce powerful results! Having a clear picture of where you want to be by next year is an important factor. If you have no idea where you want to be then it would be rather difficult to get to any destination. Take some time to figure this out. Once you do, I can promise you that applying the third level of this system will become much, much easier.

Self-Belief

There is great power in believing in yourself and the mission you have chosen to be your purpose in this life. Without this power, the time it would take to escape the depths of struggle will be a lifetime. Then after that, your release from the struggle is guaranteed because you won't have to deal with any kind of struggle again. Why wait until death claims you to finally be free? To an intelligent person like you, this may seem a tad bit drastic. However, showing it in this perspective is a guaranteed way to getting my point across.

We live in a world that tells you to believe in everything else but yourself. A world filled with perfect distractions everywhere you go. However, believing that everything and everyone else can make things happen for you is the same as sitting around doing absolutely nothing, waiting on a miracle to happen. This book is to educate you on the matters of being a "doer". The very best way of achieving anything is to invest in the power of self-belief.

Throughout time, men and women of history, who have dedicated themselves to the task of accomplishing their dream, has proven time and time again why the power of believing in yourself is crucial to becoming successful. Especially when those dark times of self-doubt creeps into your mind. This is the natural enemy to self-belief. We've all encountered those times when doubt overshadows the belief we have in ourselves.

Checkmate

This happens when we face a challenge that seems larger than we are. Since the first thought we naturally reach for is negative, we begin to doubt our own capabilities. It drains all of your creative energy from overcoming those challenges.

Those challenges can come from a decrease in your pay to making a life changing decision. But I'll let you in on a secret. There is no one who is as powerful as you in defeating your own demons and overcoming your own challenges. You will have people out there that will tell you that they can overcome your challenges better than you. However, you must not allow what they say to distract you from the actual truth. There is no way they can.

We were all created differently with different sets of skills and abilities designed to overcome our own special challenges. These abilities can only be effective when you believe in them. I'm about to be incredibly real with you. Before you go into your office of your business or the kitchen or office of your workplace, have this singular thought in mind: *Broke people have to see the results from their labor FIRST before they can believe in themselves. Wealthy people believed in themselves way BEFORE they ever saw results from their labors.* This is why it takes a lot of people so long to advance their in their respectable careers or make their businesses flourish.

Reflect on this list that you're about to read. Believe it or not, each of these points have been proven to increase anyone's success rate by 80%.

5 Golden Rules of Self-Belief

1.) **Identify and ease your doubts**.

Learning how to recognize when your self-talk takes a turn for the worse is crucial. When you hear yourself saying, "I can't," or, "I don't know," or, "What if," a red flag should go up.

Instead of telling yourself, "I can't do X," say, "I can't do X yet. But I'm working on it."

Or if you start wondering, "What if I fail?" you can respond by saying, "Then I'll try again."

Checkmate

Doing this transforms a negative situation into an opportunity for growth. In the end, it's about giving yourself a chance.

2.) **Stop listening to toxic people.**

Toxic people are convinced that everything is impossible, and they are quick to shoot down ideas. They'll poison your mind into a state of hopelessness.

Don't let them steal your energy just because they've lost theirs.

Instead, surround yourself with supportive and passionate people who can both inspire you and bring out the best in you.

They will lift you up when you feel down and help you see the bright side of your darkest fears and doubts.

3.) **Recall your successes**.

This one is tough. When you're down, you'll more easily remember the bad instead of the good. And oftentimes, the "rah-rah" pep talk just doesn't cut it.

So, I suggest writing a list. Grab a piece of paper or small notebook, or open a blank document. Now write down your successes, big or small.

If you're a bit bashful about your achievements, ask someone you trust to tell you the great things they think you've done. It's refreshing and a great confidence boost.

And finally, keep your list with you at all times. It will help you find your way back to yourself whenever you get lost.

4.) **Trust and love yourself.**

You probably spend more time being your own worst enemy instead of being your own best friend.

But you deserve to treat yourself better. After all, you have the rest of your life to spend with yourself.

Think of it this way: Would you mentally abuse or condemn your loved ones? Would you let them suffer in their time of need? If not, then why would you do it to yourself?

So, be kind to yourself. You're more capable and worthy than you give yourself credit for.

5.) **Give yourself permission to try**

Self-doubt never disappears. Over time, you just get better at dealing with it.

It will greet you every time you fall out of your comfort zone and whenever you strive to do something great.

But know that it's not something you have to fear or resent. Your doubts are only thoughts, not your future.

Sure, something may go wrong. But if you never try, you're losing an opportunity to improve your life.

Are you willing to risk that instead?

Self-Approval

Checkmate

This level is by far the most important level of the "Selfie" System you could ever master. This is what separates the mice from the men. The kitten from the majestic lion. Before you can truly start to build your legacy and rise through the ranks of your job, you must first give yourself the "ok" to do so. It is your right to grab what is truly yours. Who is to say that success at your job or business isn't rightfully yours?

The problem with most people who reside in the 98 percentage of those who work for an employer is that they believe that one cannot control his or her own destiny. This couldn't be further from the truth. You can either be one of the FOCUSED individuals (those who achieve all their goals), or one of the DISTRACTED individuals (those who are distracted by things that can never bring them success of any kind). To create an effect that can speed things along with your progress, you must approve of yourself.

Too many people wait for the approval of others before they start to believe in themselves. And it's those same people that are still waiting till this day for some sort of miracle to happen. However, the damage behind awaiting for approval from others is more extensive than you would think. How is the need of approval holding you back?

Need for approval / low performance

The need for approval is negatively impacting your performance. You tend to procrastinate, avoid doing important things, feel anxiety and fear, and get stuck in worry and rumination.

Wanting people to like you results in declining new opportunities, being too nervous to perform effectively, and showing signs of avoidance, such as apathy, withdrawal, analysis paralysis, and giving up.

If this rings true for you, focus upon how the need for approval is holding you back from doing the important things. Once you move past this, you will be free to achieve and create what you want in life with much less stress and effort, because you would be exhausting yourself through avoidance.

Need for approval / high performance

Although you're a high achiever and produce great results in your life, it is often at the expense of everything else. The need for approval in this case results in doing too much, feeling anxiety, worrying, being unable to stop ruminating about challenges, trying to please everyone, not making time for yourself, working too hard, and being unable to say no.

If this is you, focus upon how the need for approval is causing you to do too much instead of only what is important, and to do things for others at the expense of yourself.

Self-acceptance / low performance

In this instance, what others think of you has little impact on your decision-making about how to spend your time. However, your performance is low due to other motivational factors, such as being unaware of what is important to you, what drives you, and what makes you happy.

Hence, you may be stuck doing work you don't really enjoy and have habits that hinder your performance, or alternatively may not have the skills to work effectively at what you're doing.

Checkmate

If this is you, focus your energy upon getting in touch with what really matters to you. Start to listen to what you really want in your life and act upon this to make it happen. Life becomes much more effortless when you're living in alignment with what is important to you.

Self-acceptance / high performance

This is the goal I am always working toward with my coaching clients. It's a place where you make decisions based on what is right for you. You make effective choices with your time, are OK with saying no when it is required, and are committed to only doing that which is important and valuable for what you want to achieve or create in your life.

In this space, you spend much less time in your head worrying about people and situations and more time just getting things done. You don't need to be busy in order to appear successful. Instead, you choose to see success as measured by doing what matters to you and to your results. This is a collaborative space where you lead and connect effectively with others, without being at their beck and call.

The path to self-approval is relatively simple to understand. However, many can find what I am about to reveal to you, quite challenging. Just follow the steps and mastering this level will be a thing of the past.

1. *Build a sound sense of self-acceptance.*

The first step is to strengthen your core foundation so that you feel strong enough to go with what feels right for you. This way, you will no longer feel the need to look to others to feel good enough about your choices and decisions. Keep a self-appreciation journal, where you start acknowledging daily or a few times a week the things you're most proud of about yourself: choices you've made, insights you've learned, things you like about yourself, times you've stayed true to yourself, or whatever feels right for you.

2. *Let go of seeking validation from others*.

Secondly, you need to practice letting go of seeking validation for your choices and most importantly, for whom you choose to be. This means noticing your language, self-talk, and behavior, and identifying when it is coming from wanting someone else to say you're ok, that you made the right choice, or that you did the right thing.

Instead, when you do make a decision, check in with yourself that it feels right, remind yourself that it is your choice, and give yourself validation for just being you.

3. *Evaluate tasks based on approval-seeking efforts.*

Lastly, start being honest with yourself when you take on a new task or commitment, whether you're doing it because it is "right" for you or because you want to get approval and avoid disapproval.

Sit down and evaluate your weekly tasks and ask yourself what is really necessary and important, and what is driven by people pleasing. Then slowly work through the "people pleasing" list and eliminate them.

Self-Image

Here, we begin to build the image that will matter the most to you and your success. Your self-image is the person that you wish to become 5, 10, 15 years from this very moment. We've all done it at one point in our lives when we envisioned the type of person we want to be in the future. For music artists, they envisioned themselves being on stage performing in front of millions of fans before they ever left the basement. For athletes, they created their own image of receiving the MVP award before they left the field in high school.

It all begins with our inner image of ourselves. Whatever you envision yourself to be on the inside will surely reflect on the outside. This is very important when it comes to accelerating your career or your business. The most common mistake that a lot of people make is to start something without having an end game in mind. They don't have the image of the person they want to become.

It's no secret that our thoughts control our actions. Think about the last time you constantly held a thought. Examine how all your actions, from the way you dressed to the facial expressions you made, was in perfect sync with the thoughts you chose to feed energy to. This has a direct impact on how those who can provide opportunities for you view you as a professional and as a person.

Checkmate

Believe it or not, the self-image you hold for yourself has a great impact on your annual income.

This is why you see the most confident coworker earn more per year doing, basically, the same job as you. This is why you see your business rival produce more sales than your company. They both have a strong image of where they want to be financially and who they want to become. A great technique to use to boost your self-image is called the "back from the future" thinking. I recommended this particular technique to one of my clients. She wanted to become a millionaire but didn't know how to get there. So I recommended a very powerful exercise for her to do. And now, I'm giving it to you. For this exercise, have someone read this to you or go back and perform this once you understand the full concept behind it. This is how it works:

Envision yourself as a person who achieved all of your goals 5-10 years down the road. You accumulated a great amount of memorable moments doing what you love to do. The world is your oyster. Hold this image in your mind for at least 5 minutes. Within this time, think about the journey that got you to this unparalleled success. Step by step, think about the moves you made to get to where you are.

Now come back to the present. What invaluable advice would you give to your present self? What would you say? This exercise has been proven to yield great results for my client and I'm sure it will do the same for you. By the end of this exercise, you should have a great image of the person you want to be. And the bonus here is that you will have a general sense of direction you want to take.

It's amazing how the human mind works when you actually put it to work. Most would say that this is merely using your imagination. I can't deny this truth. However, imagination has been proven to create and change our current reality. Now, realize that there are two types of self-images you can create: positive and negative. Having a negative self-image of yourself will yield the same life changing potential that a positive self-image will have but in a negative fashion.

Checkmate

If you have a strong inner belief in yourself and your values, you can change your behavior subjectively by changing your attitudes of mind or your inner beliefs. This is what is known as "self-talk". For example:

You can turn a negative attitude about your weaknesses to a positive one regarding your strengths. Don't get weighed down with circumstances. The 'loser' with a negative self-image often blames others for their adverse circumstances in life and usually suffers from feelings of depression. This negative self-image then becomes a self-fulfilling prophecy, as failure follows failure in their life. So the "cycle of despair" sets in. Very hard to break out!

On the other hand, the person with a good self-image EXPECTS to live up to their expectations and achieve success, which is what usually happens. If you feel good about yourself, the brain sends out positive messages to your body. As seen in one's body language. So that you can act confidently and give off positive "vibes".

This in turn develops confidence, which makes you feel more positive about "having a go" at something you would not normally tackle. A positive attitude is absolutely essential in the path towards success in whatever endeavor in life you may choose. We all know and envy those people who project an aura of confidence and success. Don't we?

Thus, self-image is a vital self-management skill... and, like all skills, it needs constant exercise to nourish, strengthen and grow: "Water the flowers, instead of the weeds in your garden." How long has it been since we visited ourselves by looking closely at ourselves? The technical word for this is introspection. How do you see yourself now? What do you do well? What do you like most about yourself? What results or achievements are you most proud of?

Your self-image can be an 'invisible ceiling'. Don't sell yourself short, because everyone has the potential to do anything. If you can think it, you can do it. Aim high. If you train fleas to jump in a glass jar, even if you remove the jar, they do not jump any higher. Don't be a flea! Say to yourself: *"I need to lift the lid of my unlimited potential."*

Checkmate

Self-Fulfillment

We are now at the final level of The "Selfie" System. This is when we place everything together and see the results of all the other six levels. Self-fulfillment of our work is the feeling we all hope to reach some day. It's that feeling that keeps us going day by day. Deep within our hearts, we all want to do work that can provide this feeling. However, there are many people who don't realize what this level of self-consciousness means.

To reach this level would expose one's deepest desires and capacities. It brings to light what you truly would like to accomplish. I first felt this feeling when I discovered what my life's work was. It's a goal so large that the very thought of acting on it scares you. These are the goals that forces us to grow as a person and as a professional.

It is the striving for self-fulfillment which guides our lives. Have you ever worked at a dead end job and felt that "this wasn't it"? You felt as though you reached the ceiling and you have gone as far as you can go at that job. But here is the crazy thing: Millions of people still work at dead end jobs with no hope of ever fulfilling their deepest desires just to "get by".

Without realizing it, we are killing ourselves every day when we don't fulfill our intended purpose and chose to "stay safe". This level will be the most challenging for you by far. Your mission is to figure out what your intended purpose is. Is this job you're currently employed at in line with your main goal?

If so, how is it going to benefit you? The same would go if you owned your own business. Is your current business in line with your main goal? If so, what is the mission of your business? In a sense, life is entirely too short to be doing work that has no meaning. Time is our most precious commodity and once it's gone, there is no "return on funds".

Seeds of Greatness:

- ♟ **Self-evaluate** yourself on a personal and professional level. Ask yourself the hard hitting questions.

- ♟ **Self-awareness** is key to zeroing in on your true skills and abilities.

94

Checkmate

- Stay committed to finishing what you start. **Self-commitment** is the key to opening the door to success.

- **Self-belief** is the source of energy that make your dreams come true.

- **Self-approval** is knowing how valuable you are to yourself. Know where to draw the line for other people!

- **Self-image** is key to building the ultimate you! Don't corrupt the process with negative view!

- It is the striving for **self-fulfillment** which guides our lives. Lead with your desire in mind!

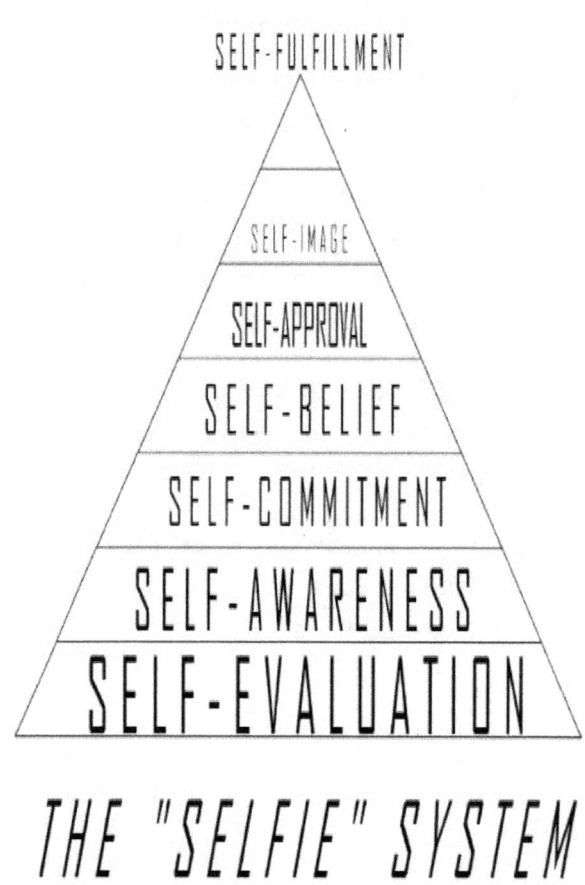

THE "SELFIE" SYSTEM

Principle 6

Dress To Impress Down To The Pen!

I found this particular lesson very powerful. You would be surprised at how many doors will open for you if you dress to impress every day! People will literally treat you differently than if you were to walk around in some jeans and a t shirt. For example, I went to the bank one day to inquire about a financial consultant. I had my suit on at the time because I had a prior business engagement. When I walked in, the service I received was entirely different than what I normally would have gotten if I had walked in with some casual clothes on.

At the end of the visit, not only did I receive the information I wanted in the fastest way possible, but I also was informed about a deal they had when their app first came out. I got an extra 10 dollars from it! They even offered me a service where I can receive a $200,000 loan! Another great example happened when I had on a suit when I walked into one of my favorite restaurants.

As I was waiting on my order, a businessman was sitting at a table across the way from me. He glanced at me and asked what it was that I did. I explained to him that I decrease stress and raise workplace morale, creativity, and overall workmanship causing a 52% rise in profits and productivity as a success expert and influential speaker. By the expression on his face, you could tell he was blown away. He stated that it was nice to see a young man such as myself dress so nicely and run a fully functional business.

He was impressed to say the least. He even told me about some opportunities and people he knew that would help me spread the word about my business and book in San Diego. Now I was blown away!!! Dress to impress and even wrap yourself with a bow. You may never know who could be watching you. Remember, if you run a business or just looking for employment, your image is everything.

Not only does this boost your self-confidence, but it also boosts your chances of obtaining more business or job opportunities you never would have seen coming. Represent yourself in the very best way when out in public and when on the job. This includes the pen you use as well.

For many of those who run a business, the pen is a very important piece. This fact falls true especially when you're sitting down with a client and you're at the moment when you're about to close the sale. All there is left to do is the signing of the contract. If you take out some cheap Papermate pen, it would show the customer that your business is still new and that you're a rookie at best. This could affect the outcome of the sale. I speak from experience when I say that this is true.

I lost a very great deal due to the pen I gave for the signing of the contract. It's a hard lesson learned but helped me to realize that you really do have to dress to impress down to the pen! The very next day I ordered a custom made pen with my initials on it. My success rate of sales went up by 48%! During my interviews with different CEOs, they have all concluded the importance of proper presentation and the pen is a part of that.

If you have an office job, this concept applies to you as well. If your desire is to climb to the top of the ladder at your workplace, take this lesson to heart. While most bosses won't check out the labels on your clothes. Unless you have an extremely high-profile job where fashion is everything. The way you dress will likely make an impression on your boss no matter where you work. Looking presentable is very important.

Waking up and throwing on clothes without thinking about what you're wearing won't score you points. Certain factors including how your clothes fit, which colors you wear, and how much skin you show, can affect how other people perceive you at work. Neat, presentable work attire can help you move up in your career, or at least keep your job, while consistent inappropriate clothing may negatively affect the way your boss perceives you. Particularly if your company has a dress code, breaking it can mean bad news for you. Thankfully, you can dress to impress if you follow these five easy steps that was provided to me by a retired CEO.

Think about those who will see you

It's common to hear people say to dress for your day, and this is awesome advice. Dress for your day implies that you should do just that; if you're sitting at your desk all day and your company allows jeans, then that might be just fine. However, if you have a meeting with an important client or your boss, you might want to dress up in a nice suit, or at least business attire.

Regularly thinking about the people who will see you will show that you care about your job, and that you take it seriously. Many people also say that you should dress for the job you want: this means that even if everyone else in your job class wears jeans and polo shirts, you might want to dress a little nicer. Go the extra mile. Very few travel down that road.

Be neat

Obviously, if you work at a fast-food restaurant with a required shirt, you won't have a lot of options besides possibly which black pants you wear. However, you can control how neatly you dress in any situation. Tuck your shirt in, and make sure you wash it regularly. It doesn't matter if every other person you work with is wearing the same shirt as you; if your shirt is clean and tucked in, and some of your coworkers' shirts are ripped or dirty, you will be the one looking more presentable.

The above analogy is true for more than just a job at a restaurant. Looking neat and presentable is important for any job. Many workplaces are now encouraging a regular casual dress code; although you may be allowed to wear jeans, that doesn't mean that you should wear jeans with holes in them. You can be neat no matter what you wear. The same is true for a business suit: a business suit isn't impressive if it doesn't look neat and well-maintained.

Look sharp

In addition to dressing neat, you should dress sharp whenever possible. This comes back to the idea of dressing for your day, but you can look sharp even on your relaxed days. You don't have to spend tons of money to look sharp, either. While fancy name brand clothes make a nice touch, they aren't always necessary, and for some jobs, they aren't even appropriate.

One way to dress sharp is to have your own unique style and to maintain it. This doesn't mean that you should dress so absurd that everyone in your office knows it's you even without seeing your face, but having a clear personal style is a good thing as long as you're being respectful of your work culture. Avoid tacky additions that take away from your clothing, or focus your coworkers' attention on your clothing instead of what you're saying.

A great example would be a ridiculous looking tie or an absurd colorful blouse. One last way to dress sharp is to keep in mind what is appropriate for the season in which you're working; if it's winter and thirty degrees, don't come into work in a sun dress or shorts. You know, the common sense stuff.

Wear the right size

This seems like it should be the most obvious advice on this list, and yet many people fail to wear well-fitted, appropriately tailored clothing regularly. Tailoring your clothing is a great way to look sharp at work, but even if you choose not to tailor your clothes, you should still try to find clothing that fits properly.

Coming into work with clothing that is too big makes you look lazy, and sometimes gives the impression that you don't care about your job. On the other hand, wearing clothing that is too tight can distract your coworkers. One study found that risqué dressing at work is improper for all jobs; managers who dressed in a sexy manner were seen as less intelligent and competent.

Remember the details

Even if you wear clothes that fit and are fashionable, you will undermine all your hard work if you don't pay attention to details. For women, this often means wearing minimal makeup, and both men and women should brush their hair if they have longer hair and wash their face, etc. There are also many items that you should avoid at work, including baseball hats, pajamas, offensive t-shirts, clothes with holes or rips, clothes that show too much skin, and so on.

Checkmate

Also, when possible, think about the colors you're wearing. Many people believe that dark colors make them look more professional, but color can be fun and appropriate if you make careful choices. Red can appear scary or send a bad message, blue can be calming, and other colors send different messages as well.

Red is the color of energy, passion, action, ambition and determination. It is also the color of anger and sexual passion.

Orange is the color of social communication and optimism. From a negative color meaning it is also a sign of pessimism and superficiality.

Yellow is the color of the mind and the intellect. It is optimistic and cheerful. However it can also suggest impatience, criticism and cowardice.

Green is the color of balance and growth. It can mean both self-reliance as a positive and possessiveness as a negative, among many other meanings.

Checkmate

Blue is the color of trust and peace. It can suggest loyalty and integrity as well as conservatism and frigidity.

Indigo is the color of intuition. In the meaning of colors it can mean idealism and structure as well as ritualistic and addictive.

Purple is the color of the imagination. It can be creative and individual or immature and impractical.

Turquoise is communication and clarity of mind. It can also be impractical and idealistic.

Pink is unconditional love and nurturing. Pink can also be immature, silly and girlish.

Magenta is a color of universal harmony and emotional balance. It is spiritual yet practical, encouraging common sense and a balanced outlook on life.

Brown is a friendly yet serious, down-to-earth color that relates to security, protection, comfort and material wealth.

Gray is the color of compromise - being neither black nor white, it is the transition between two non-colors. It is unemotional and detached and can be indecisive.

Silver has a feminine energy; it is related to the moon and the ebb and flow of the tides - it is fluid, emotional, sensitive and mysterious.

Gold is the color of success, achievement and triumph. Associated with abundance and prosperity, luxury and quality, prestige and sophistication, value and elegance, the color psychology of gold implies affluence, material wealth and extravagance.

White is color at its most complete and pure, the color of perfection. The color meaning of white is purity, innocence, wholeness and completion.

Black is the color of the hidden, the secretive and the unknown, creating an air of mystery. It keeps things bottled up inside, hidden from the world.

The most important thing is to make sure that you know the dress code at your work, and to dress appropriately for whatever you have going on during a particular day. If you want to go further than that, be sure to look sharp, and if possible, *dress for the job you want instead of the one you have*.

Checkmate

Seeds of Greatness:

♟ Represent yourself well by dressing well. On and off shift!

♟ The pen matters!

♟ Colors spark emotions in others. Think of that the next time you get dressed.

♟ Keep a clean and neat appearance. It's the center stone of how others view you.

♟ Wear clothes that fit. Yes. It does matter!

Principle 7

Mapping Your Professional Network

"No man is an island". I don't know who said those words but I do know that there is wisdom within them. Networking with other people is essential when it comes to building a solid business and building a solid foundation for your career. This technique of sorts has been the sole source of business for centuries. Depending on the types of professionals you have within your network will determine the success percentage of your career or business.

Think of it this way: there are thousands of people who participate in network marketing businesses for years, but don't know how network marketing really works. We tend to forget what the term "network" defines. Build solid relationships with other people! It's all about the relationships and trust you build with thousands of other people. Strangers may find it hard to do business with you but your friends may not. This is what networking is all about.

I want you to imagine, if you will, going out and meeting new people every day. There are billions of people all over the world who may share the same interests as you and there are those who don't. However, this is to your advantage. Because when you build your network with people who may not want to do business with you, but may know someone who does, you win. Remember, it's not always about who you know, but who they may know.

Making connections and maintaining relationships with the people who support you throughout your career can be the key to success for most individuals. By effectively building a network of colleagues, business associates and more, you're ensuring that whenever you need a new client, a new job, or to develop your skills further, you can call upon your network to help you out.

Networking is perhaps more crucial than ever as an established relationship can make you stand out against the competition. For anyone who has ever worked as an intern at a large organization, one of the best pieces of advice you'll receive is to network with friends, network with other professionals, and network more while you're there. Take advantage of the access you've been given, go out of your way to meet other intelligent individuals and build up a network of contacts so that when you leave or when they leave, there is a foundation for a relationship in place.

Within this chapter, you're about to learn what the different categories within your network of contacts are, how to best utilize some of the greatest features on LinkedIn, and why face-to-face networking also known as "in-person" networking is still the best.

Networking Categories

Back when snail mail was the main form of business communication, it could take days to establish a connection with someone from another company. With the creation of the telephone, professionals gained the ability to just pick up the phone and call someone to make that contact. Today, technology has, in many different ways, made even telephones unimportant. With only a person's name, you can Google search them, look at their LinkedIn profile, observe their Facebook information, and, if they tweet, then their Twitter stream.

The availability of information on people has drastically improved, but it doesn't take away from the importance of old-fashioned offline networking. If you ask ten different people to define networking, you'll get ten different answers. But according to The Oxford Dictionary, a network is "a group of people who exchange information, contacts, and experience for professional or social purposes."

The real definition of networking is building relationships before you need them. It's difficult because we tend to only do things in life when we need to. But if you're running a marathon, you don't wait until the morning of the race and then just go out to run. On that day of the race, you remember all of the time and hard work you put in ahead of time while training to get to that point. With networking, when you really need a job or new clients, empowering your existing contacts is the key to getting you there.

When considering your contacts, Darling recommends that you think of them as five different subgroups within your network, try not to interconnect and view it like an inverted pyramid.

Database: Everyone in your contact that you've interfaced with via email, phone, speaking engagements, rolodex, Twitter, this is the largest group.

Network: Your friends and family network, alumni network, or business network. These are specific sub-groups but people you trust. They should rarely go over 200 contacts, and to determine if someone is in your network, consider if they would immediately return your phone call. If they get back to you, then they are in.

Inner Circle: Ideally about 50 people who can rotate annually and give you candid career feedback about your career. Darling likes to put together a survey at Surveymonkey.com every two years so these people can give her honest thoughts without fear of offending her.

Personal Board of Advisers: 5-6 individuals you're particularly close with and who should be your go-to network for advice that not only touches on your career, but on you. How are you doing as a person?

Friends, Family and Fools: The most obvious group, these are people who probably like you because they either have to, or they just do.

How to Network Effectively: Social Media Networking

While networking has always been vital to business relationships and growing a client base, it's never been quite as easy as it is now. While face-to-face-interaction remains the best form of networking, you no longer need to rely on snail mail or even phone calls to interact and create a group. With social networking sites, you can research and connect with other professionals easier than ever. And the leader is LinkedIn, an eleven-year-old business-oriented social networking site. This is called hybrid networking; so taking the online to the offline; digital relationships to face-to-face meetings.

Launched back in May 2003, LinkedIn has seen its biggest growth the last few years. It has gone from 30 million members and 200 employees in early 2008 to over 75 million worldwide members and over 600 employees, according to company spokesperson Krista Canfield. Additionally, a new member signs up for LinkedIn every second of every day, and the users span 200 countries worldwide.

There are plenty of additional options out there for social media networking. But the real value of LinkedIn lies in using it to discover the hidden connections between your network and the rest of the world. There's not a lot of social tools or games, which is good because you won't get lost in all the features as you may on other sites. But to be successful on LinkedIn, you must have a completed profile and have some sort of an effective strategy.

Checkmate

According to a recent report from Nielsen, Americans now spend more time using social networks and online games than they do e-mail. Back in June 2009 alone, U.S. Internet users spent about 22.7 percent of their online time on social networking sites, up from 15.8 percent just one year ago, the report said. But there are tips and tricks to using LinkedIn, beyond simply creating a profile and connecting with contacts, is to get the most out of your experience.

Utilize LinkedIn's Features

If you've joined LinkedIn but haven't filled out any of the more detailed descriptions of yourself, you're not getting the most out of the network. It's all about engagement in the community. And the more complete your profile is, the more that potential clients, HR managers and friends can learn about you. If you think about it very simply, your LinkedIn profile is search engine optimized (SEO), so the more information about your background, the more recommendations you've received, and the more quality contacts you have, the less barriers there are for a stranger to learn about you.

Checkmate

But there are some additional tools on LinkedIn you should take special note of to optimize your experience.

Avoid Generic Requests: One of the biggest mistakes you can make on LinkedIn is to send a request to connect with a former colleague or business partner but without thinking about personalization.

It bugs the heck out of me when I get an email that says 'Please Join My Professional Network'. I feel as though that if you couldn't even take the time to change one word in the invitation, why should I accept the invite? Always personalize your invites. It will pay off sooner than you think.

Mind Your Online Manners: Your LinkedIn network is not the same as your Facebook friends or Twitter followers. This should be strictly a pure business connection. So think about what you're saying and posting before you put the information out there. While some of your friends might be intrigued to know that you had undercooked meat for lunch and would never go back to a specific restaurant, is that something your business contacts need to know?

117

Checkmate

Think about managing your network and groups like you would handle yourself at a business lunch. If you wouldn't go into lunch announcing that others should buy your product or service, don't do it in a LinkedIn group. Think about how you would feel if you were in someone else's shoes and you saw that post.

Quality Not Quantity: While certain sites like Twitter may be more about quantity of followers, LinkedIn should really be looked at as a home for quality connections. It really is about having those personal relationships. There are people on LinkedIn called LION users (short for LinkedIn Open Network), who will accept connections with nearly anyone without really having a true relationship.

Slow it down a notch and don't try to meet the entire world on LinkedIn. If you have 5,000 people in your network, it's not humanly possible to maintain that network well. It's the same way with networking. Spend extra time on the people you actually know.

Checkmate

Follow Companies: For those familiar with the Facebook model where you can become a fan of a page or organization, it's quite similar but with a lot more benefits. By following a company like Apple, Microsoft or others, you can see status updates from that organization just like you would get from a person, including company news, new hires, departures and job listings.

With LinkedIn's degrees of relevance, you might be surprised to know who in your network knows someone at that company or can put you in touch with the client or hiring manager for a position. Additionally, if you're a small business, you can actually see what people are following your company.

Search Your Competitors: This skill is certainly not specific to LinkedIn, as you should constantly be monitoring what your competitors are doing. Not just companies, but individuals. If you work as a vice president of sales, do a quick search by title to see what other people with the same title have done with their LinkedIn profiles. You can see what is working for them, where they've been and more. That can in turn help you to make the most out of your profile, but more importantly maximize your value to your company.

Join Groups: Create them, join them and just get involved in them. Depending on your industry, there are plenty of groups that gather professionals in your field from similar positions and companies who you might not know. Users can click on the Groups tab at the top of the LinkedIn homepage to search groups formed around interests, industry or careers. As a group administrator, you can send out announcements to everyone in your subset or just read what others are up to.

Importance of Offline Networking

While online networks have certainly changed the industry and made it much easier to meet contacts and stay updated on their status and career news, nothing will ever touch the offline impact of face-to-face networking. The most obvious places you can network offline include "networking" events, conferences and more. And while many view conferences as an opportunity to learn information about new technologies and companies, it's also a great networking opportunity. And technology can help you both before and after the fact.

Usually when I go to a conference or networking event, I'm able to research the speakers and attendees online and see who I'm most interested in talking or listening to. In years past, you were stuck with a pamphlet and a three-line bio of folks, but now you can find out so much more. If it's someone I'm really interested in, I'll send them an email ahead of time with the header 'Look Forward to Meeting You at the Conference' and try to set up a time to talk. I found using this particular way of doing business most effective.

Once you're actually at the event, the art of swapping business cards is just as important as it's always been. You can share your information with someone in just an instant, and many of the more creative individuals are including more than just basic information these days. Some people even put their own photo on a business card, which is great in helping others remember who you were.

Checkmate

Again, technology and smartphones have made swapping information at an offline event easier than ever. With an innovative new app for the iPhone and Droid operating systems called Beam Technology, you can literally bump your phone with another person's and instantly your contact information is transferred. This includes info, pictures, calendar events, and even social network connections like LinkedIn.

But once your information has been exchanged, it's vital you focus on engagement once you're home from the conference. Send a personal message to tell them how great it was to meet them, set up a time to meet again if they're in town, or join groups that they are a part of to engage in conversation.

Effective networking is all about the people you know and meeting new people through other people. Your network is only as strong as the way you manage it.

Principle 8

Who's Really In Charge...

For the world of me, I couldn't figure out why some people rose to the top of a company faster than most. Then one day, it donned on me like a sunrise on a Saturday morning. With any service or product that we provide, there will always be a customer whom we serve. This is the person who pays all your bills. This is the person who gives you money to buy that brand new car of yours and the house you live in. If you please them, the more money you will receive.

In today's world, many people have forgotten the true nature of building a fantastic career or a booming business. We've lost touch with what's truly important. We live in a world where technology is ever growing and the closest we get to human contact is through text message or social media. Customers are shopping online more and more with each day that passes by.

For those of us who work in retail have forgotten that the best way to rise to the top is to provide the customer with a "once in a lifetime" experience every time they walk through the door. I once remember having this conversation with a dear friend of mine about the importance of providing a great experience for the customer. All people except a special few have forgotten what makes customer service such an amazing experience. The happier they are, the more you'll see of them and the more money they will put out. This works well within the boundaries of the Law of Equal Exchange. The type of experience that you provide the customer with will determine the compensation that you receive.

You could very well be the high spot in that person's day. Think of it this way: What kind of experience would you like to have if you walked into a restaurant or a store? Then simply provide that experience to your customer. One of my clients used to work as a waitress. For a week, I sat in the restaurant and watched her work. She did a great job except that she did the bare minimum. She got their food to them in a timely manner and filled their drinks when needed, but has no soul when doing so. When she received little to no tips for her services, she would get upset and wonder what the problem was.

I asked her to put herself in their shoes. If she was her own waitress, would she tip high? There was no experience provided. I recommended that she had more fun when interacting with her customers. Become the reason why they would return. Smile more, get to know their names, have fun with them, and of course take their orders. Make it a personal experience for you and your customer.

Usually, job training wouldn't teach you this aspect of waiting. A few weeks later, we sat down for a final consultation. She had this most amazing look of excitement on her face. She informed me that ever since she worked on "becoming the experience" and applied that to her work, her income jumped up! She went from receiving $2 tips to $15-$20 tips within 3 weeks!

Checkmate

She is now the most talked about waitress at that restaurant and because of her style of waiting, it even bought more customers there. She is now running her own waitress training business that is bringing in an upward amount of $200,000 a year. Not a bad outcome for someone who started out as a waitress. The spirit in which you give your service is more important than the service itself. When you apply a positive attitude to your work, positive circumstances begin to happen. There will be days when customers with the nastiest attitudes will walk in. They may have had a horrible day up to that point.

Do not allow their current attitude to effect yours. Still provide the experience. Perhaps their attitude will lift by your positive vibes. You'll never know who you're entertaining. It may be a person who is looking for someone like you for their business and willing to pay top dollar for your services. This is the secret to growing your business or taking your career to the next level. It is those who are the most talked about in a positive way that get promoted and paid more.

I realize that not everyone who picks up this book will deal with outside customers.

However, there is another customer that must be pleased as well. This is the person who gives you your paycheck twice a week. This person would be your boss. Within this type of workplace, treat your boss like they are the customer. Give them the experience of how it feels to have someone who works for them that they can trust to get the job done. Think of it this way: If you were the boss, what type of person would you want on your team?

Become that person and watch how more responsibilities are placed on you. The more responsibilities you have, the more valuable you become and the more you're paid. People tend to shun responsibility and think it would mean more work. However, going the extra mile will bring more fortune your way. It's been a proven fact for centuries. Look at the person who does a little more and watch closely to what happens. You will see that what I say is true.

Every day is a new opportunity to change your life. If you had been waking up, dreading to go to work, then now is a good time to change your experience. Your experience at work is completely up to you. There will always be people who would see to it that you're just as unhappy as they are. The only question you must ask yourself is: *Will I allow someone else to create my experience for me?* Those who take control of their lives control the outcome of all situations and circumstances. Remember that a job is only a stepping stone to your greatness. Learn from the job to eventually move to bigger opportunities.

Seeds of Greatness:

♟ Become the reason why customers return and they will become the reason why you attain success.

♟ Treat your boss like they are the customer.

♟ The spirit in which you give your service is more important than the service itself.

♟ Your experience at work is completely up to you

Principle 9

Work Survival 101: Becoming The Asset

There is simply no other way to say it. So I'm just going to give it to you straight. No one is going to pay high for someone who has little to no value to them. There are many people who actually believe that they can get something for nothing. This is also a part of the Law of Equal Exchange. Within the marketplace, the services you render or the product that you may be selling must hold some type of value.

If you're providing a service or product that isn't in demand, you will see little to absolutely no profit come your way. Your bank account will be very empty. However, if you have something that is unique, the people see as a valuable asset, and you can market it well, you are well on your way to wealth.

So the question now is, how does one increase their value? You have the right book, at the right time, in the right moment. Because it is here that you are directly involved with self-development. Self-development is key to raising one's value. To develop yourself is to obtain new skills or hone in on skills that you already have and increase your knowledge base. By doing this, you are actively taking control of your own income.

There are many of those who believe that if you work really hard at your job, you will get promoted faster and earn more money. Taking that route, you might get a few pennies added to your paycheck, but nothing that will make you a highly paid superstar.

Working really hard at work will win you the employee of the month, but it won't make you a real superstar and that's why we are here right now. To point you in the right direction to obtain your massive millions. When you work harder on yourself than you do at your job, you're increasing your value to the higher ups.

The same thing goes when you're running a business. Working on yourself on a daily basis will open more doors and opportunities for you and over time increase your income. Since you are your business, it stands to reason when you're developing yourself, you're developing your business.

This is extremely effective when you're dealing with a network marketing business. People respect and pay for *VALUE*. People within companies are divided into assets and liabilities. You do not want to be among the liabilities (those who cause trouble without profitable reward).

With this principle, you will learn how to show your value. It's time to put up or shut up and in today's world, you cannot hide your value and expect your business to flourish or your career to take off.

Once in an interview with the CEO of Unlimited Minds, Inc., Brian Tamers, he gave me an impressive list of effective tips for anyone to survive in a company. He told me that, "if anyone would commit these tips to memory, their time in a company would be a successful one." Here is the list:

"The Big 20"

1) **Shut up and listen**. If you don't know what you don't know, then seek out some experienced advice. A mentor can warn you about things you may never have considered and keep you from being blindsided by unforeseen events or costs. As hard as it may be, the first step is to admit to yourself that you don't know everything.

2) **Avoid your workplace troublemakers**. Often there are no greater timewasters in the workplace than your fellow colleagues. There are the colleagues who love to gossip and spread rumors. The colleagues who are constantly trying to catch your mistakes. The office flirt who will only get you in trouble. And the bad news bear who doesn't want to do

anything but bring you down with bad news.

3) **Don't be afraid to abandon ship**. Be flexible when it comes to your career path, even if it means changing careers midstream.

4) **Recognize "deal or no deal" situations**. Don't be afraid to walk away from deals that just can't seem to come together.

5) **Constantly add value**. Companies are in the business of making money. To a certain extent, we all have to pull the company line and help keep the revenue machine running. Make sure that you continually add value to the company.

6) **Sing your own praises, but not too loudly**. As a general rule, your work won't speak for itself. You must speak for yourself. There is nothing wrong with tooting your own horn here and there.

7) **Get smart-err**. Too many people don't understand the basics about the operation of their companies. Learn the organizational chart and reporting structures. Study and understand your company's financials.

8) **A minute wasted is millions lost**. The most valuable commodity you have is your own time. Spend it wisely. For example, don't invest eight hours in putting together a presentation when you can deliver the same results with only an hour's prep time. Management wants the content of your message, not a bunch of fluff and pretty artwork.

9) **Be a confident innovator**. When you pitch your ideas to management, be prepared to defend your views. Also, be prepared to receive criticism.

10) **Nip it in the bud.** People tend to emphasize negative things in the workplace over positive things. One negative person or event can tear

down months of motivation in minutes.

11) **Don't ask for more than you truly deserve**. American corporations seem to have become the land of entitlement where people expect to be highly compensated before they have provided one penny of value to the company.

12) **Don't be afraid to say no**. That is, if you're doing such a great job your company can't afford to get rid of you anyway. If you don't set limits, you will find yourself working on a perpetual treadmill.

13) **Trust your intuition**. Good intuition in the business world can be your guardian angel. If it feels like someone is up to no good, she probably is.

14) **Seriously, get a life**. It's good to be committed to the company, and corporate accomplishments are

rewarding, but when all is said and done, a lifetime goes by too fast.

15) **Know which position on the ladder is right for you**. Do you want to be responsible for the success or failure of your company? If so, move up the ladder. Do you want to go home at five every day and forget about work until the next morning? Then moving up the ladder is not for you.

16) **Don't be tempted by a shiny new title**. A bigger title usually comes with a pay raise and more perks, but some companies have discovered that a simple change in title with few additional incentives is enough to keep a person motivated.

17) **Learn the difference between e-communication and real communication**. Communicating with people is an opportunity not only to transfer information, but also to build

relationships with them at the same time.

18) **Add sales to your skill set**. You are your own boss in reality. Despite what your resume says, adding sales to your skill set is a must. Whenever you're trying to pitch a new idea to your company, you'll have to have a sales pitch that is convincing and sound. And if you are vying for a promotion or raise, you'll need to be prepared to pitch yourself.

19) **If it isn't broken, don't fix it**. In business, change can often be confused with progress. Often you'll find that companies are making changes and improvements for the sake of change – and not because anything was truly wrong in the first place. You will notice that employees feel the pressure to constantly make improvement to things to keep up the appearance of productivity and to prove their worth. Pointless really…

20) **Be a part of the bottom line**. If you want to be valuable to your company, then you need to contribute to its bottom line. In other words, you need to help it make money (the asset). Otherwise, it's not worth it to your company to keep you around (the liability). Make a concerted effort to connect to what it is that makes your company money, and focus on the talents and skills that you have that will contribute to those things.

Needless to say, but we'll cover it anyway, you can use these same tactics when it comes to running your own business. Tailor these steps as it fits into your plan. To tie this up, your main objective is to simply focus on what you need to get done to ensure your productivity. This is basically what most successful people do at work.

I'm pretty sure that most of these steps that you read, you've seen people around you do the exact opposite. Shortly after the interview with Brain, he gave me one of the major keys toward becoming successful. With a smile on his face he said, "To become successful, you just need to slightly outthink everyone else." Everyone else works hard on the job for their money and rarely receives a raise.

You will work hard on yourself to increase your value to earn more money. Rather it be at your job or your own company or small business. The choice is entirely up to you. Keep in mind that these are simply suggestions. But if you want to see results, these are the guidelines that will help you see your massive success. Where ever you may wind up.

Seeds of Greatness:

♟ Working on yourself on a daily basis will open more doors and opportunities for you and over time increase your income.

♟ To develop yourself is to obtain new skills or hone in on skills that you already have and increase your knowledge base.

♟ People respect and pay for *VALUE*.

Checkmate

♟ You cannot hide your value and expect your business to flourish or your career to take off.

♟ To become successful, you just need to slightly outthink everyone else.

♟ Be a part of the bottom line. Period!

Principle 10

Those Who Master Their Time...

Life is nothing more than time you spend on this earth. It is our most precious commodity and unfortunately for a lot of people, the most wasted. A lot of people in our world today spend a lot of time watching television, talking on the phone, reading up on what is happening in celebrities' lives and so on.

Doing these things will not only stop you from living life, but will kill any hope of you fulfilling your true potential. For those looking to succeed, you must put in the time and effort. Without using your time correctly, you're running out of that essential time needed to make your dream a reality. I can tell you this, you won't reach it watching television all day.

With walking the path to success may come great sacrifice. There may be some things you enjoy doing now that you may have to put off until you have reached that goal you wanted to achieve.

For many of us, we enjoy going out to clubs, parties, etc. But is this taking up time that you could be using to getting closer to your dream? Is this a distraction to your income? The answer to these questions would definitely be a *yes.* It is known that many people wasted their younger years partying instead of moving forward to making their dream income.

Therefore, wasting the precious time that they will never get back. Time is money. This is a simple saying, but true none the less. Each minute that goes by is another dollar one could have earned. If you want to be successful, you must prioritize what is truly important to you. Is partying every weekend now helping you to get closer to your goals of obtaining massive success? It is way more fruitful to put in the time now and party later when you have succeeded in your goals of making more income. There is a feeling of peace of mind when you go out at that point.

Another waste of your time is watching television the entire day. There is an entire life out there waiting for you to take hold of. If you invest your time in doing nothing but watching the tube now, expect nothing later on. Many people complain about how they wish they can make more money and be wealthy like the top 1%.

But they do nothing more than that. They go home and watch reality shows of billionaires and the wealthy. As they are watching, they are wishing that they can live the life of a superstar. This simply won't do if you plan on achieving anything.

Your situation today was based off of decisions you made yesterday. If your decision is to wait for something miraculous to happen to you, you will always be in that state of waiting. It won't come for you I promise. You won't meet your goals by doing that. You must put in some of the work if you want to meet your success in the middle.

Checkmate

Success is attracted to those who are hungry for it. Success is also granted to those who invest the time into it as well. In other words, success is not bought with money, but with your time. This goes into that phrase, "you reap what you sew". The seeds you lay down today will grow with the time you put into it.

Later on down the line, those seeds will have grown into massive success, if you take care of those "seeds" properly. Time management is crucial to your success and should be taken very seriously. It would help if you knew how to manage your time correctly. Well you're in luck!

In the following example, I have provided you with 30 tips you can use in which to manage your time better. However, these are only suggestions. But if you want to be truly successful, it would be wise to take heed.

1. **Make a to-do list (electronic or paper).** Put the most important item first and work down from there.

2. **At the end of your day, review what you've done and make a new list for the next day**. In order of importance.

3. **Be ruthless about setting priorities**. Make sure that what you think is important is really important.

4. **Learn to differentiate between the important and the urgent**. What's important is not always urgent. What seems urgent is not always important.

5. **Carry your to-do list with you at all times**.

6. **All things being equal, do the hardest, least fun thing first.** Just get it over with!

7. **If a task takes less than five minutes, do it right away**. If it takes longer, put it on the list.

8. **Deal with E-mail at set times each day, if possible**. If you need to check messages as they arrive, limit your sessions to less than five minutes.

9. **Schedule some uninterrupted time each day when you can**. Concentrate on important tasks, even if you have to take refuge in a conference room or at the library.

10. **Another approach**. Before you check your E-mail or voicemail or get involved in the minutiae of the day, devote a solid hour to your most important project.

11. **For a couple of days, take an inventory of how you spend your time to find out where and how you're wasting it.**

12. **Eliminate the time wasters** (e.g., if personal phone calls are taking up too much space in your workday, turn off your cell).

13. **Cut big jobs into small chunks**. Order the chunks by importance. Work on one chunk at a time.

14. **For big, complex tasks, schedule wiggle room.** Projects tend to take longer than you think/hope. Give yourself a buffer.

15. **If part of your day involves routine repetitive tasks, keep records of how long they take and then try to do them faster.**

16. **Go one step further and set specific time limits for routine tasks**. Work tends to fill whatever amount of time you happen to have.

17. **Establish smart efficient systems for all your tasks, big and small, and stick to them.**

18. **Value your time**. People who wander into your workspace to chat do not respect you or your schedule. Set boundaries.

19. **When and where you can, say no**. Trying to do everything everyone asks you to do is a recipe for failure.

20. **In general, guard against over scheduling yourself.**

21. **Bottom line to items 19 and 20**: Learn to delegate, wherever and whenever you can.

22. **Aim to handle pieces of paper only once.** Same for E-mails. Read them and deal with them.

23. **Reward yourself for completing tasks on time.** No fun stuff until the work stuff is done.

24. **Organize your workspace**. So you don't waste time looking for things.

25. **Schedule demanding tasks for that part of your day when you're at your peak.**

26. **Group related tasks** (e.g., sort papers on your desk and then file them). It's more efficient.

27. **Use down time** (e.g., waiting for meetings to begin) to, for example, update your to-do list or answer E-mails.

28. **This advice applies to life outside work, too.** It's better to be excellent at a few things than average at many.

29. **Don't be afraid to get projects done early**. It takes them off your mind, and it doesn't mean you'll just be given more to do.

30. **Create the business environment that works for you**. Adjust the lighting, turn off your E-mail notifications, and get that cup of coffee. Set the stage and get to work.

Principle 11

Profit Within The Problem

Within any type of workplace, there will always be a time when problems come up in a moment's notice. We tend to allow these problems to overwhelm us, thinking that those problems will endanger the business or our very own careers. Could it be that problems only exist to teach a lesson that can send our businesses or careers to the next level? Quite a thought isn't it? Throughout history, those who ever did anything of note viewed their problems in such a light that rarely anything could stop them from accomplishing their goals.

Usually within the workplace, very few bring up the problems alongside with a solution. Very many see problems as an unsurmountable barrier and it's "beyond" them to solve it. However, to reach the level of the high performers, one must see the profit within the problems.

"Within in every problem, there is profit. Either you learn how to win or you learn how not to win. Either way, you profit."

You see, those who can access a problem will eventually find the answer to it. Most of the time, the answer is right in front of us. It just takes wisdom to see it. No matter what circumstance or problem you may come up against, you will learn something when it's all said and done. When that happens, we grow as individuals, therefore profiting from the experience of going through the ordeal. I was raised with the solemn belief that everything happens for a reason.

Life will throw the most complicated challenges your way. The more complicated they are, the more you'll profit from the experience you gain. The more experience you gain, the more valuable you become to those around you. This is no different at your job, no different than the problems that you encounter in your business, and definitely no different that the challenges you encounter while on the journey throughout your career. What I'm saying is this: Look forward to problems coming up and adjust to those problems as they arise.

Thomas Edison is a great example of what I mean when I say "profit from the problems". This man failed to create the florescent light bulb 9,999 times! To him, it didn't matter that he kept failing. For he knew that every attempt that he made toward achieving his goals was well worth it. When he finally achieved his goal, he was asked by a reporter, "Why didn't you give up?" Mr. Edison replied, "For I learned 9,999 ways how not to make a light bulb!" He still profited from all the problems that arose during the creating process! Unsuccessful people believe that one must avoid problems. Successful people look forward to them so that they can perfect their work!

Usually when you try to avoid all your problems, you wind up in a worse position than you were in before. And what happens when you wind up in a worse position? We try to avoid the problems that come along with being in a new position. You might as well grab a shovel and keep digging. There is no money in avoidance and definitely nothing to gain. Here is a few tips to how you can profit from problems that arise at work.

Acknowledge that there is a problem

We've all been down the road where we would rather ignore the problem and hope it goes away. We rather think that there is nothing wrong than to except the truth of the matter. However, the problem will still be there tomorrow and the day after that and so on. What you ignore will continue to grow until you face it.

Dissect the problem

Once you acknowledge the problem, begin the process of dissecting it. If you dig deep enough, you will find the origin of the problem and figure out a way of solving it.

Learn from the problem

Within every problem is a lesson to learn. You're a little wiser for it too. Now that you faced your problem and fixed it, it will be easier to solve similar situations in the future. If the problem becomes costly, you now have a way to prevent it from happening in the future which will save you money in the long run. This is where you want to be.

Your value has raised

You're now more valuable to your company. If you keep going down this path, you will become the go-to person. This in turn will make you look good to those who matter. This will increase your promotion rate by a whopping 40%!

Most problems are unexpected, but that doesn't make those problems any harder to overcome. If you move swiftly and don't procrastinate, you will discover that problems can go away just as quickly as they arrived. Let's take this subject and view it in another perspective. This is what you will need in order to move to the top of the chain. Very seldom do the person who solves most problems stay at the bottom for very long. Think about the best car mechanic in the city. Chances are high that they will earn more per year than the mechanic that gives horrible service and cannot fix any issue with your car.

This builds a reputation. The word reputation is very powerful. This will determine whether or not you become a massive success or a massive flop. By solving most of your customers, clients, or boss's problems, you build a reputation of being the best. This is what you should focus on. Be the problem solver that always have the answer. And even if you don't know how to solve the problem, that's ok. Be the person that can find the answer or at least know where to look to reach a solution. Remember this quote, apply it to your overall service, and you will look like a superstar to your customers, clients, or boss:

"If you bring up a problem in one hand, have a solution ready in the other. One should never come before its counterpart."

In other words, don't bring a solution to something when there is no problem (this will cause a problem) and don't bring a problem with no solution in mind (the problem will grow and cause more damage). This is the key toward bumping up your pay in within the first year. I want you to concentrate on building up your reputation of being the go-to person for answers this year. Chances are high that by doing this, you will see the profit of all your hard work in the following year. When reaching this module in my program for my clients, we perform an exercise that trains the mind to find a solution to the problem before bringing it up at work.

I instruct them to think of problems and solutions as husband and wife (you decide who plays which role). One should never come without the other. You would be surprised at the success rate that most people have within their job, career, or business when they enter into this state of thinking. Now you have the tool that will take you to the next level and over time, will produce the fruit that will change your lifestyle forever.

Seeds of Greatness:

- Within in every problem, there is profit. Either you learn how to win or you learn how not to win. Either way, you profit.

- Life will throw the most complicated challenges your way. The more complicated they are, the more you'll profit from the experience you gain. The more experience you gain, the more valuable you become to those around you.

♟ Acknowledge that there is a problem

♟ Dissect the problem

♟ Learn from the problem

♟ If you bring up a problem in one hand, have a solution ready in the other. One should never come before its counterpart.

Principle 12

Check List: Your Greatest Tool

Setting a checklist on a daily basis is a handy tool that will help one build great momentum within the workplace. It has the similar effect of drawing out a map to reach your destination in the most expedient manner. There are many CEOs, supervisors, managers, and other highly paid people out there who use this tool to get what they want done. For example, many businesses work off of a systematic process that helps "recruit" new people or helps one make the maximum amount of sales that can be made.

Checkmate

In the network marketing business of Organo Gold, they have what you call the "4 Steps". It's a 4 step process, if followed to the letter, will help anyone who is new to the company to see immediate results. It's in the form of a checklist.

Checklists have been the focal point to many who have set the standard to achieving their own personal success. It is a powerful tool to have indeed. However, the reason why others don't utilize this tool that would help them to accomplish all their tasks set for that day, is that most are afraid that having a checklist would be too overwhelming.

Using this tool will help you better organize your tasks and to keep record of the tasks that you have already completed. This is to help prevent the overwhelming factor. My mentor once told me that there was a reason only 3% of people control 97% of the money and why 97% of people fight for 3% of the money. Those 3% knew what they were doing and knew where they were headed by using a checklist.

There may be some challenges to creating a checklist. Many would argue that one may not know what to do to get to their goal. So how would you write down tasks if you have "no knowledge" on what it takes to get to that point? The "K+I (2) =(X)" formula that was introduced in my earlier work, The Blueprint to Success, play quite a role in this. You don't have to be a genius to figure out what to do. Just simply use your know-how that you possess already. And with a little imagination and initiative, you created an effective checklist.

I have no doubt that even Bill Gates himself had to utilize one of these to build his massive empire. One cannot hope to reach higher pay and a larger income bracket of this magnitude without it. "Rome wasn't built in a day". However, something as simple as a checklist can be. Take some time the night before to write down all the things that need to be done for the next day. You tend to feel a sense of satisfaction when you complete a task and are able to check it off of your list.

One shouldn't allow doubt to interfere with this step onto success. For doubt will only ensure that you stay right where you are. I too once had this problem. For the world of me, I couldn't grasp the concept of creating a checklist. At the time, I couldn't understand how that would affect anything. I was sure that it would only waste my time. Boy, was I wrong!

Once I decided to give it a try, my entire world changed. I started to see that things that I was putting off or just kept forgetting about was finally getting done. It was amazing to say the least. I used this checklist method to pick up rank in the military. It isn't until you decide to do things differently that your life is experienced differently.

At the risk of sounding silly, I do believe it was the checklist that lead me to my calling in life. It was the power of the list that lead me to write three books prior to this one. It was the power of the list that lead me to building my company as well. To build a company that I can use my gifts and talents to help people grow in their businesses was a task on my personal list. I wish I could share the feeling that I had with you when I finally checked that task off my list.

What is it that you aspire to be? What is it that you aspire to obtain? What are you willing to do to get there? To ensure that your list yield results to you, you must apply the "GPS" system to it. What is this system that I speak of you may ask? It is broken down into three tasks that must be done in order to see that your checklist comes to past.

The "GPS" System

Goal Setting- involves establishing specific, measurable, achievable, realistic and time-targeted goals. Work on the theory of goal-setting suggests that an effective tool for making progress is to ensure that participants in a group with a common goal are clearly aware of what is expected from that. On a personal level, setting goals helps people work towards their own objectives.

It is considered an "open" theory, so as new discoveries are made it is modified. Studies have shown that specific and ambitious goals lead to a higher level of performance than easy or general goals. As long as the individual accepts the goal, has the ability to obtain it, and does not have conflicting goals, there is a positive linear relationship between goal difficulty and task performance.

Goals are a form of motivation that sets the standard for self-satisfaction with performance. Achieving the goal one has set for oneself is a measure of success, and being able to meet job or career challenges is a way one measures success in the workplace or life.

Persistence- firm or obstinate continuance in a course of action in spite of difficulty or opposition.

Sacrifice- to give up something important or valued for the sake of other considerations or rewards.

Simply put, achieving your goals won't be an easy journey to take. But it will be well worth the effort that you put into it. So starting your own journey checklist will give you the control over your future and how it plays out. If you're seeking wealth, one must undertake the task of building an empire to do so. So seriously, what are you waiting for? What are you willing to do to ensure that you gain everything you want?

Checkmate

Principle 13

Multiple Streams of Income

For many of us, we've heard the same ole tired line from our parents (those who aren't rich or even close to being financially free), friends, and the rest of society: *"The way to live your life comfortably is to go to school, get good grades, and get a good job with benefits.* Is this similar to what you've heard? This is one thing I know for sure: Whoever said that was an evil genius. It was a great way to keep people within the "employee" mindset for most of their lives.

Honestly, who would want to move up or raise the standards if all you thought you had to accomplish was those three tasks to live life with options? It would be really hard to break that mindset if you've been raised to

163

believe in that. We begin to learn and develop habits at a very young age. We imitate everything that our parents did and everything that they believed in. We began to weave their beliefs into our very own.

What if I told you that there is a way you can begin to live your life in such a way that you can choose to stop working for weeks and still be financially stable? Sounds like a fantasy right? I can ensure you that this is the truth and we see people do it every day. However, given what's on television every single day, a lot of people fall into the belief that you would have to be a celebrity or a famous athlete to make it big. We also tend to fall into the thought that all you need to do is find ONE source of income and you can become financially free that way.

This won't cut it in the real world. One very important factor that I taught my clients is that financial stability plays a very big role in our peace of mind. When I asked some of my client's what they thought multiple streams of income were, they told me that they thought it was having more than one job. Unbelievable. For the great majority of our lives, people actually thought that the way to financial freedom was to work for more than one "boss". In fact, the only thing that this would do is drain your life away.

You would literally be trading your TIME for MONEY. You would be trading your MOST PRECIOUS MOMENTS for MONEY. And if you look around, you would notice that a lot of people are living their lives this way. You must realize that this is the quickest way to become a zombie. Yes, zombies are real indeed.

It's the look a person has once their spirit is crushed, their dreams demolished, and their time wasted. If this is the way you feel about your life right now, it's time for a change. Within the majority of this book, you've learned what it takes to navigate your way through the workplace and make a strong impression, take your career to the next level, and how to build or rebuild your business by using a different foundation to support it. However, now I will show you multiple ways you can generate income that will change the way you experience life forever. Now, before we dive right into the multiple streams that will generate passive and residual income, I would like you to ask yourself this question that will challenge your beliefs in how money works.

Are you working hard for the money or is your money working hard for you? Take some time to do a complete inventory of your life up to this point. Are you using your job as a stepping stone to greatness? Is your career your true life's calling? Is your business your soul child or are you just using it as a means to bring in money? The main concept here and the key to attaining financial freedom and generate wealth is to have the money work hard for you. Your money doesn't require sleep. It doesn't have to skip holidays and miss time with the kids.

If you see money as an end to your means, you miss out on life and all the great moments it provides. If you see money as a tool that can work for you instead, you can have all your holidays, spend more time with your family, and "ball out" as much as you want. To grasp the concept that I'm giving you, think of all the famous billionaires today like Donald Trump and Warren Buffet. What we see now is that these men have all their fingers in different pies. Warren Buffet invests in many different companies by stock trade. Donald Trump has multiple businesses that each generate a substantial amount of money for him.

And what do they do with that extra money? They invest in another company's stock or invest in opening another business venture. Get this: neither of them don't require them to be there! This is the true way to building financial freedom and accumulating wealth. The problem that most people have is that the reason they don't start this chain of investments lie in the fact that they don't know how or where to start!

Here is the secret: all you have to do is start. A person wouldn't think of looking up the recipe for an apple pie if they had no intention of baking one. The same thing goes for building multiple streams of income. A woman wouldn't think of looking up the recipe for building wealth if they had no intention to do so. So now I'm sure you're reaching a point to where you would like to learn how you can make money work for you.

This is the part where you should open your mind to the possibilities. It took me awhile to learn this simple truth myself. It was only after I spoke to many different CEOs and my millionaire mentor that I learned what it took to become wealthy. It went against everything I was ever taught. You see, the media will only show you the lifestyles of these famous millionaires and billionaires as they are now. However, to figure out how they got to that point, you must go back to when they had nothing at all and do exactly what they did step by step.

So now that we got you in the correct mindset to receive this information, let's dive right into it. I sat down for an interview with a local multi-million dollar, retired CEO of a very profitable company here in San Diego and she gave me the secret behind her wealth and how she built it from the ground up. To maintain her wish for privacy, I will refer her as "Mrs. CEO".

Interview:

Q: Ok Mrs. CEO, could you please explain the importance of passive income?

A: Well Lorenzo, creating genuine passive income is the holy grail of personal finance. Not all passive income is created equal mind you. Some streams take much more initial effort to start, such as saving enough to buy your first rental property. But once you start it's very difficult not to gain momentum.

Everything passive first takes active energy. The time to put in the effort is when we are young and not ravaged by disease or burdened by family obligations. I remember being able to snowboard from 9am until 4pm every day for a year. Now, I'm lucky to last from 11am until 2pm without wanting to go to the hot tub and drink a bucket full of beer! If we can appreciate how lucky we are when we are young, we'll be able to maximize our vitality and live financially freer when we are older.

With sustainable passive income, you can retire early and travel the world, start a business in a field you're passionate about, stay at home to take care of your family without having to worry about money, find a job that pays less, but is more interesting, volunteer for causes you truly care about, be a big brother or big sister to those who need a role model, spend more time with your parents, sit in a coffee shop on a 80 degree day in Paris for hours on a Wednesday afternoon, eat tapas and drink sangria until 1 am on a Monday evening, potentially live longer due to much less stress, and experience perfect endless summers over and over again.

There is so much you can do once you generate enough passive income to pay for all your living expenses. I highly encourage everyone to at least try. Lorenzo, I will provide for you the framework in which you and anyone you deem fit to share this information with can create passive income success. I'll also provide an update on my estimated 2013-2014 passive income streams which have grown since retiring in 2012.

Q: Wow. That sounds great. I'm sure the information you're about to provide will help millions change their lifestyles forever! How do you start generating passive income?

A: Save like nobody owes you anything! Passive income starts with savings. Without a healthy amount of savings, nothing works. Your overall "Money Strength" will be an F- if you do not build a financial egg. In our current low interest rate environment, you must save even more than before. It's important to also realize that the savings I am referring to is the after-tax savings.

You need to save money after contributing to your 401k and IRAs since you can't touch pre-tax retirement accounts without a penalty until 60. Ideally, everyone should max out their pre-tax retirement funds first, but if you don't have enough funds and want to retire earlier, then a decision to have more accessible post tax money will still work.

Q: How much did you save and how much are you saving now that your plan is working?

A: Well Lorenzo, I saved 50-70% of my after tax money, after my 401k contribution every year for 13 years because I knew I could not last in finance for more than 20 years. Now I am saving 100% of my passive income as I try and bootstrap my online businesses.

Q: That seems like quite a task! What do you do next?

A: **Find out what you're good at!** You see, everybody is good at something. Be it investing, playing an instrument, playing a sport, communications, writing, art, dance, and so forth. You should also list several things that interest you most. If you can combine your interest plus expertise, you should be able to monetize your skills. A tennis player can teach tennis for $65 an hour. A writer can pen her first novel. A finance buff can invest in stocks. A singer can record his first song. The more interests and skills you have, the higher chance you can create something that can provide passive income down the road.

Q: Interesting. I preach this all the time to my clients and my audience when speaking. What are you doing to create your passive income?

A: Lorenzo, two of the things I love to do is write and invest. Combine these two interests with my ability to get things done equates to multiple investment types. I understand why some writers go crazy. There's so much information in my head that I need to write it down or else I might explore. Surely, being a writer yourself, you can understand what I go through.

Q: Indeed I do! It got to the point where I must carry a small journal with me everywhere I go for fear that I may forget all my "at the moment" ideas! Now, Mrs. CEO, if you would be so kind to tell me what the next step is to building this framework you spoke of.

A: **Create a plan.** It was Mark Spitz that once quoted, "If you fail to prepare, you're prepared to fail." You must create a system where you're saving X amount of money every month, investing Y amount every month, and working on Z project until completion. Things will be slow going at first, but once you save a little bit of money, you will start to build momentum. Eventually, you will find synergies between your work, your hobbies, and your skills which will translate into viable income streams.

Q: This is pure gold Mrs. CEO. Please tell me, what did you do or are still doing to create your plans?

A: I'm very glad you asked me that Lorenzo. I use one of my sites to write out goals like, generating $2,000,000 a year working 4 hours a day, trying to make winning investments, and keeping track of my passive income streams. My site and the community helps keep me accountable for progress. It's important I do what I say, otherwise, what the hell is the point? You should consider starting a site or at least a private journal. Write out your specific goals, tell several close friends, and stick to the plan.

Q: Would my blog, The Coach's Corner, be like the site you just mentioned?

A: Not at all. You use your blog to help people grow by providing wisdom. The site I'm mentioning is like a checklist that everyone can see and be inspired by.

Q: I see. I never thought about creating such a site before. Perhaps I should. Thank you for the tip! Now, how does one view this in such a way that one can stay interested?

A: **Treat passive income like a game!** The only real way to begin your multiple passive income journey is when you're making active income. The initial funding has to come from somewhere. Hence, treat passive income as a game that has various levels. If you fail to achieve one level, it's not the end of the world since you still have active income and can restart. Furthermore, a game is meant to be played with integrity. Using shortcuts such as non-passive income streams, someone else's income as a supplement such as your spouse's, or one-offs like capital gains does not count. The primary purpose of any game is to bring enjoyment to the player and beat the boss.

Q: This sounds interesting. What are you doing to win this said "game"?

A: Lorenzo, I view passive income as funny money to keep myself sane during this long journey. I estimate 2-10 years to get to my goal depending on how active I am. The dollars created are just points one can accumulate. I've made passive income goals for each passive income type and check in at least once a year like I am now to make sure I'm on track. Passive income is also carefully managed to minimize tax liability. When you can build a buffer for a buffer, you're then free to take more risks.

Q: This interview is getting better and better. Let's keep going and dig in deeper to discover your secret toward creating passive income. What's next?

Checkmate

A: **Determine what income level will make you happy.** Think back to when you made little to no income as a student. Now think back to the days when you just got started in your career. Were you happy then? Now go over every single year you got a raise or made more money doing something else. How did your happiness change at all, if any? Everybody has a different level of income that will bring maximum happiness due to different desires, needs, and living arrangements. It's up to you to find out your optimum income level.

Q: How did you decide what your income would be?

A: I first identified my favorite places in the world to live like San Francisco, Honolulu, Paris, Amsterdam, New York City, and Lake Tahoe. I then looked up the median rent and housing prices for each city. Then I factored in private education costs for two kids to be conservative. Given, I may not have two kids and public schools are often good enough. After calculating all vital costs, I then did a self-assessment of how happy I was earning $50,000, $100,000, $150,000, $200,000,

Checkmate

$250,000, $300,000, $350,000, $500,000, and $750,000.

I decided working 20 hours a week making $200,000 a year is the best income balance for maximum happiness.

Q: I've never thought of it that way before. It seems as though that would be a great way to gage what you want your annual income to be. How do you determine worthwhile passive income streams?

A: **Always remember that everything is relative.** The best way to determine worthwhile passive income streams is by comparing the likely return (IRR) with the current risk-free rate of return. If I round up, the 10 year bond yield is at 3%, any new venture should thoroughly beat 3%. Otherwise, you're wasting your efforts since you can earn 3% doing nothing.

Q: What is a realistic goal for you while doing this?

A: My realistic goal is to have a blended annual return of 2x the risk free rate. With a current 6% hurdle, I am not paying down mortgages that cost less than 5%. Debt at 6%

is a wash. My realistic blue sky scenario is 3-4x rate of return over the risk free rate. Which can be achieved with property, stocks so far for the past five years, and certain private equity investments.

Where I am dragging is my blended average CD interest rate of roughly 3.75%. Its guaranteed money, but one of my biggest goals is figuring out how to reinvent this large egg starting in the next two years.

Q: So what is the biggest downfall you see from people looking to build passive income?

A: **Never ever withdraw from your financial egg!** The biggest downfall I see from people looking to build passive income is that they withdraw from their financial egg too soon. There's somehow always an "emergency" which eats away at the positive effects of compounding returns. Make sure your money is invested and not just sitting in your savings account. The harder to access your money, the better. Make it your mission to always contribute X amount every month and consistently increase the savings amount by a percentage or several until it hurts.

Checkmate

Pause for a month or two and then keep going. You'll be amazed how much you can save. You just won't know because you've likely never tested savings limits to the max.

Q: How did you set up your investment accounts?

A: Well Lorenzo, I've set up multiple investment accounts outside my main operations bank that deals with working capital e.g. checking, and paying bills. By transferring my money to fidelity, Motif Investing, and two other banks as soon as it hits my main bank, I no longer have temptation to spend on frivolous things. As a result, I can wake up 10 years later and reap the rewards of compounding. My 401(k) is the best example where constant contributions over 13 years has grown to almost half a million without any savings pain given. It just became a part of life. Real estate is also a fantastic asset class for the long term.

The transaction costs make trading inefficient. Sooner or later, your financial egg will grow large enough that it spits out difference making income. Once you get to that level, you will be more inclined to save more. It's like finally seeing results in the mirror after working out. There's just no going back to flab.

Q: I see. This is a powerful set of habits to take on to build the framework for passive income. Is there anything else you would like to add?

A: Yes. **You must force yourself to start!** "A journey of a thousand miles begins with a single step." Laozi was a great philosopher who penned this popular English translation. Everything great started somewhere and you must set aside one day to tackle your financial independence goal. Circle the date on your calendar and cancel all other distractions. Although starting is most difficult, once you do the inertia of your efforts help carry you forward. Action arises from stillness.

Q: This is so true. I often tell my clients that the key to success is taking the first step toward it. What was your experience when you first began?

A: The first two years was brutal while I lived in New York City. I told myself there was no way I could work on Wall Street for my entire career because I'd probably die from heart failure by age 40. Having an early death in my mind willed me to save 50%+ from the first year onward and devise a CD, real estate, and stock investment distribution system for my savings every year. I thought about starting my site for at least a year before I hired someone from Craigslist to set me up and push me forward. Hiring someone to get started is totally worth it if you're a master procrastinator.

Failure is a part of life. I'd rather fail a hundred times and learn from my mistake than never try at all. Whenever I'm fearful of trying something new, I remember back to my youth when I did not ask a girl out or when I didn't try out for the varsity basketball team. These two things might sound silly to you, but to me, I use them as reminders to stop being afraid. Embarrassment, failure, and loss of money is much better than regret.

Q: Great information! Now let us move on to your passive income snapshot.

A: I use Personal Capital to track all my finances in one place. It's much easier to use their free software to follow 28 accounts on one platform than to log into various accounts to check my balances. The financial egg that can be assumed from this income stream is roughly $3.15 million dollars if you take $110,216 divided by a blended net annual return of 3.5%. I'm very focused on stable, low risk returns. To get to $200,000 a year in passive income at 3.5% means I need to grow my financial egg to roughly $5.7 million. The passive income stream excludes my online active income which itself has a business value as well as private equity investments which do not pay any income.

Financial Samurai Passive Income Streams

Category	Monthly Passive Income	Yearly Passive Income
CD Interest Income		
Bank 1 CD 1	$943	$11,316
Bank 1 CD 2	$350	$4,200
Bank 1 CD 3	$94	$1,128
Bank 2 CD 1	$778	$9,336
Bank 2 CD 2	$482	$5,784
Bank 3 CD 1	$160	$1,920
Online Bank 4 Savings 1	$41	$500
Total CD Income	**$2,848**	**$34,184**
Dividend Income		
Company Stock	$633	$7,596
After Tax Portfolio	$335	$4,020
Pre Tax Portfolio	$866	$10,392
Structured Notes	$210	$2,520
Total Dividend Income	**$2,044**	**$24,528**
Real Estate		
Rental Property 1	$1,560	$18,720
Rental Property 2	$1,050	$12,600
Rental Property 3	$425	$5,100
Total Rental Income	**$3,035**	**$36,420**
Other		
HTEYL Book Sales	$1,200	$14,400
P2P Lending	$57	$684
Total Alternative Income	**$1,257**	**$15,084**
Total Passive Income	$9,184	$110,216
Goal By June 2015	**$16,667**	**$200,000**
Deficiency	$7,483	$89,784
Source: FinancialSamurai.com 2013		

Checkmate

CD Interest Income: The reason why there are so many CDs is because I'm a rate seeker. Banks are always offering different promotions and it's up to us to move our capital accordingly. My six CDs have been the same for the past several years because they are all 7-year term CDs yielding between 3% - 4.2%. The last one was taken out two years ago.

Every year the CD portfolio grows by over $30,000 meaning I get an additional $1,000+ in interest income a year due to compounding. I plan to only renew my CDs if I can find a 7-year yielding CD for 3% or higher. Capital One 360 with no fees has an interesting savings program with an APR of about 0.75%. I like how I can fund excess liquidity by just linking my checking account.

Dividend Income: The S&P 500 grew another ~20% while dividend payout ratios held steady or increased. As a result, my like-for-like dividend income has also grown by around 20%. The financial sector gained roughly 28% in 2012 which is especially good since I have a lot of deferred stock in my old financial firm. I think dividend income will continue to grow given public companies have record cash on their balance sheets. They need to either mobilize their cash through investments, or return cash to shareholders in the form of a buyback or dividend payout increase.

I invested a large chunk of change in several structured notes in the summer of 2012. The yield to maturities range from two years all the way up to six years. The structured notes are a way to play the upswing in the stock markets while providing downside protection. For example, a large investment was in a Dow Jones structured note at 12,400 that provides 100% downside protection, 115% participation (15% outperformance kicker), but only a 0.5% dividend yield vs. a market dividend yield of around 2%. I'm happy to give up 1.5% in dividends per annum for six years to ensure my money will be there when the note expires.

Finally, I still advise those who are in the earlier stages of their investment careers to focus more on growth stocks vs. dividend stocks. It's all about building a large enough capital base so you can generate large enough dividend income. If you're a 30 year old and buying Walmart and Coca Cola, you'll probably do OK in the long run, but you aren't going to see huge outsized growth because these companies are already quite mature. My main goal in investing is capital appreciation and not dividend income at this stage.

Real Estate: This is where things got really good and why I continue to love real estate. I was able to get a free loan modification for one of my vacation properties out of the blue in January 2013 that lowered my payment by $670 a month. Meanwhile, HOA expenses declined by $80 a month, yielding $9,000 a year / $750 a month in extra cash flow. The other good news is that rents have gone up by roughly 5% on this specific property. I also raised my main rental property's rent by 11% and my other rental property's rent by 4%.

Other: It took me four months of absolute focus and two years of data to publish my first e-book last summer. The book went through over 30 revisions by four people. The second half of 2012 was my testing period to get feedback from readers and fix any mistakes. The distribution channel is only here and through a couple affiliates. For the next 12 months, I plan to reach out to at least 10 new relevant sites to write guest posts or do book reviews. Income should continue to grow given there is no other book out there that teaches you how to profitably quit your job by negotiating a severance package.

In the fourth quarter of 2012, I also started investing with Prosper.com. I'm starting slow given I've got a year before my first CD rolls off. I look forward to generating realistic 5-8% returns vs. their advertised 9%+ returns. If I can gain the confidence in putting my entire CD allocation into P2P lending, such passive income could double to over $60,000 a year.

Hopefully my passive income chart provides you with a good snapshot of how various passive income streams can really add up over time. As part of the passive income framework section, I set out a goal to make $2,000,000 a year working four hours a day by December, 2018. In twelve months, I was able to grow my passive income stream from ~$80,000 to ~$110,000.

Despite the passive income increase, there is roughly a $7,400 a month / $90,000 a year passive income deficiency. Below are some thoughts on how to achieve my goals.

Q: Would you please give us some ways that we can benefit financially.

A: Allocate CD Income to P2P Lending: P2P lending returns should be able to return 5-7% in a relatively low risk way. Take a look at the various interest returns by credit score and borrower rating in this post. I'm comfortable starting off with $10,000-$20,000, but I don't have the guts to invest hundreds of thousands of dollars yet. However, if I study P2P lending over the next two years, perhaps I will have the confidence to at least lob $250,000.

The $250,000 would see a roughly $8,500 incremental annual income increase if I could get 7%. I recommend starting off with $2,500 and 100 notes average $25 a note for diversification. Build your portfolio as you gain more confidence.

Continue To Raise Rent & Refinance: Real estate truly is my favorite investment asset class. Unfortunately interest rates have ramped higher by 1% from its 2012 lows so I probably won't be refinancing for a while. San Francisco rents grew by 15% in 2012 and I expect them to grow by at least 7% in 2013 and another 7% in 2014 due to the surge in internet/technology business. Such rental increases will lead to $5,000 a year in additional income.

Meanwhile, my mortgage interest payments continue to go down by an estimated $42,000 a year as principal gets paid down, leading to a total positive swing of $7,000-$8,000 a year in profits. Put it another way, if I can pay off all my mortgages I will generate an incremental $42,000 a year in cash flow. If inflation picks up, then the figures should go much higher.

Book/Product Sales: I'm happy to sell 30-40 books a month at $48, but I've been thinking about raising the price since I think it provides so much value. How much would you pay to gain back your freedom and walk away with thousands, if not tens of thousands of dollars and do what you've always wanted to do? To me, freedom is priceless. But of course I'm biased about how good my book is and should also consider decreasing the price to see if there is elasticity of demand. I will continue to build up relevant articles about career development, severance packages, entrepreneurship, and so forth. I can see book sales double off this low base due to an increased effort in marketing, leading to an additional $18,000 a year in passive income. Maybe I'll even write another book!

Municipal Bonds: I've been fearful of municipal bond funds for a while given what's going on in Europe. Thankfully, muni bond funds have now gotten hammered thanks to a drastic rise in interest rates. I'm going to spend a good amount of time researching any laggard muni bond funds with tax free yields of 4% or greater. If I can allocate a third of my CD money in muni's, I should be able to easily beat a 4% gross return (2.8% net at a 30% tax rate) since muni bonds are tax free and regularly yield over 4%. Muni bonds could generate an incremental $5,000 a year, however, I could also easily lose principal value.

Checkmate

So far, I've come up with a realistic way to generate roughly $33,500 – $38,500 a year in additional passive income in two years. Unfortunately, I'm still $55,000 short of my $200,000 a year passive income goal! I'd like to continue keeping my estimates conservative in nature because it's better to end up with too much than too little.

Q: What about other sources of income?

A: As part of the passive income framework section, we are playing the game with integrity. It's no fun beating the Big Boss with a cheat code or super weapon that annihilates all enemies with one click of a button. The goal is to develop income streams that keep rolling in if we do nothing at all!

Q: What income streams don't count?

A: *Capital gains*. Unless you can repeatedly sell stock for profit, capital gains is a one off item. It's just as easy to lose money in the markets as it is to make money, so stop pretending like you're Warren Buffet.

Freelance writing. Quality freelance writing takes tremendous effort. Ironically, the better the quality of your writing, the more you don't want to freelance and just keep the articles for your own site. Freelancing is a great way to earn side income, however, it's not really for me. I'll probably take on one or two freelance jobs maximum per year and write no more than four articles a month elsewhere.

Financial Consulting. $1,250 for the FS Steele Package requires hours of preparation before the three calls and hours of preparation after the call to make sure there is follow through. Furthermore, a client gets five comprehensive e-mail consultations in between sessions which takes time as well. Consulting is very rewarding because there's nothing better than helping someone understand things. It just takes a lot of preparation because I want to give the best, most tailored advice to my clients as possible.

Selling anything. If I decide to one day sell my rookie card for $800, I'm not going to include this in my passive income streams because I've only got a couple of them. Same thing goes for selling a watch or electronic device.

Checkmate

Blogging. Content does not magically appear out of thin air as some might believe. It takes a tremendous amount of effort, consistency, and creativity to come up with helpful and interesting content. The only people who really appreciate how much it takes to be a blogger is another blogger, not even a freelancer. We've got to take pictures, edit, market, build a brand, guest post, and network. Compare this with our journalist friends at any other major media publication who get to write assignments, submit and be done with.

It's easy to get lazy if we do not compartmentalize our income streams. We must be honest with our income streams so our income can be honest with ourselves."

After this interview ended, I had a new sense of financial knowledge. We all have goals that we want to reach. There are many people who wish to create success in more areas than just their job, career, or business. With this information, I hope that you put it to good use. Knowledge without practical use is nothing more than useless trivia.

Principle 14

The Power of the Sale

"The key to success in accumulating a larger annual income is simple. It happens when one person takes money out of their pockets and places it into your bank account in exchange for a product or personal service". The chances are great that most people who are reading or read this book, are not great salespeople. It's more accurate to say that most people dislike the image of going door to door trying to sale a product or service.

More people would say that they possess no skill in selling at all. This simply is not true. The fact is that everyone sells. Rather it be an idea that you are trying to get across, or persuading others to do what you want. This art is one of the most powerful arts to learn.

Checkmate

And with this principle, you will do just that. Most times, we all sell ourselves without realizing that we are. When most businesses start the recruiting stage, the "scouts" find out that a lot of people often use the excuse of not knowing how to sale most of the time.

You will hear phrases like, "I hate sales" or "I just don't have the salesman spirit". This is nothing more than fear and uncertainty speaking on the person's behalf. It is studied and proven that most successful people are salesman. Similar to the "Art of War", the art of salesmanship can be mastered and will provide you with the financial freedom that you seek. To further prove my point, look back on all of those who have obtained great wealth and status.

You have people like Bill Gates, Warren Buffet, Magic Johnson, Oprah Winfrey, etc. who went from nothing to multi million and billionaires. How do you think they obtained the golden goal that so many are striving to reach? If it wasn't them selling, it was someone else who did. Salesmanship plays a great part in our daily lives. Take notice to your actions the next time you try to convince someone of your ideals or when you at a job interview. In order for others to support your ideals, you must know how to properly sell your ideas. In order for that employer to hire you, you must convince them that you are the better choice over your competitors.

For most people, this art is feared. People simply don't like to be told "no" or rejected. My millionaire mentor once confided with me that "once people get over this fear and learn that those "no's" will eventually lead to a "yes", they will increase their annual income by great numbers". This has rung very true in the course of my life so far. By understanding this concept, you are close to obtaining a lifestyle that very few managed to accomplish and becoming much more valuable to your respectable market. Thinking in such a way can lead you away from your initial comfort zone.

There are three keys to becoming a great salesperson. You must be trustworthy, assertive, and optimistic.

Being Trustworthy

•**Put the customer or client first**. You can't sell anyone anything if they don't trust you. Convincing someone that they need someone requires that you balance sincerity with your desire to make the sale, being assertive, firm, and honest. If they don't trust you, they're less willing to make an intelligent buying decision.

•**Empathize**. Find out what your customer/client really wants and why they want it. People buy "things" as a means to an end. Understanding your customer's desires and adopting them yourself will make you a great salesman.

•**Allow your customer to lead interactions, and ask questions to determine their desires**. If a customer says they want a suit, ask "What's the occasion?" Selling a suit to someone going to a funeral is a lot different than selling to someone who is celebrating a recent promotion.

•**If a customer expresses interest in a particular item, ask what it is they like about it**. Allow them to choose the product that they feel good about, getting to know your customer and their taste, and uncovering their real motivation for buying.

•**Be an expert in your field**. Know everything there is to know about your product, and your competitors products, so that you can justify to your customer why your recommended product is the right one for them. If you're selling basketball shoes, learn which players wear what shoes, what styles are collectible, and some of the history of the shoes. Likewise, learn all the technical details about sizing, comfort, and care for the product.

•**Follow up**. If you really want to be a great salesman, go the extra mile. Write down the names and contact info of your customers, and follow up with a brief call or note to make sure they are 100% happy with their purchase. This is how you turn customers into raving fans who will return to you in the future. This is how you get referrals from your customers, and promotions from your employer.

•**Look the part**. There's no particular style-- a car salesman will probably dress somewhat differently than a salesperson at a guitar shop--but you need to figure out how to look as appropriate and approachable as possible. Be clean, appropriately groomed, and friendly.

Checkmate

Being Assertive

•**Anticipate objections**. Pay close attention to your customer's reactions. Facial expressions and body language can be a big "tell" in the customer's attitude. As you pitch the product to them, remember that you are there to sell whatever is going to make the customer feel really good about their purchase. Guessing what part of the product or price the customer is objecting to will help you respond tactfully and persuasively. If a particular product seems to turn off a customer, acknowledge it rather than starting to argue for the product. You might objectively name some of its merits while justifying the customer's hesitation: "It is more expensive than the others, you're right. The hand-stitching takes a lot more time to complete, but it results in much more durable shoe."

•**Be logical**. If you're working on commission, it can be tempting to always up-sell, or try and get customers interested in the most expensive items. But trying to up-sell a big screen plasma TV to someone living in a dorm room that isn't big enough for it is likely to put your customer off of your sales style.

Balance your desire to make a sale with what product makes sense for the customer.

•**Ask for the sale**. If the customer is having a difficult time making the decision, it's ok to do a little pushing. Trust that you have suggested the best item and ask something like "Would you like me to bring this up to the checkout stand for you while you continue your shopping?"

•**Increase your units per transaction**. After you confirm a sale, make the case for add-ons to up your total sales. If you've just sold a printer, mention some deals you're running on ink cartridges or reams of paper. Frame it as a money and stress-saving measure for them: "You'll need these eventually and this way you won't have to worry about it."

Being Optimistic

•**Forget bad sales**. Spending lots of time on a sale that falls through can be frustrating and discouraging, but learning to put bad sales behind you and quickly approach new opportunities afresh is the best way to become a more successful salesperson. Treat each failed sale as practice. What did you learn from it?

•**Stay focused on your own sales**. Some workplaces try to stimulate sales by encouraging competition among the sales staff, posting numbers for the week or the month. While this can be a friendly way of selling enthusiastically, it can also be discouraging if you constantly compare yourself to other salespeople.

•**Keep busy**. The more sales you attempt, the easier it will go. It'll be much easier to get past small failures and little setbacks and will keep you honing your craft. If you're making calls or roving the sales floor, the day will likewise go a lot faster the more time you spend selling and making your profits.

•**Blame nobody**. Whatever happens, avoid placing blame anywhere. It's ultimately the customer's decision whether or not to buy something, so don't treat it as a failure on your part if they choose not to. Think of yourself as a counsellor in a transaction. Make your suggestions, be as helpful as possible, and move on when the deal is done, successful or not.

Always remember, you are here to serve and help your customer or client. Listen to everything that he or she says carefully, and listen to exactly how they say it. This is your fire power when presenting the product as a solution, and you want to present the solution back to them the same way they presented the need to you.

You must also tailor your pitch to the customer. People like different things. All the bells and whistles are just noise unless they're ringing their tune. The last bit of advice of honing in on your art before we move to the next section is to always be a person of integrity, because they will be able to see if you are not.

The Challenge for You

This is your challenge: I challenge you to do better than you ever have done before. Go the extra mile and become a better competitor by becoming a better person.

Realize that, in life, we are always in a state of learning. Lessons don't stop after schooling. It rarely does. You have so much unlimited potential to become greater than you are now. God made sure that He created creatures with unparalleled power and unlimited growth potential.

Know that there is no such thing as an "uncontrollable destiny". It's not time that controls our end result but what we chose to invest our time in that determines our ultimate outcome.

Be the savior of your own life by becoming the miracle for others. Energy is always perpetuating in a full cycle or circle. What you put out to the universe and what you do for or to other people will surely come back to you twice as powerful.

Do the "impossible". Impossible is just another way of saying "I'm possible". There is nothing that God throws our way that is impossible to handle. If it's happening, there is a purpose for it and a lesson to learn. Either you grow from it, or allow it to destroy you. Remember that only you can **ALLOW** things to happen **TO** or **FOR** you.

Principle 15

The Master Key

I started an experiment on my life based off of a theory that I came up with to see what results I would get from it. After a few weeks of bringing positive energy to all my situations, shortly after realizing what negative and neutral energy does, I have discovered a fundamental truth that has truly changed my experience in life and produced results far from what I'm used too. I had an "ah ha" moment that changed everything.

At many points in our lives, we encounter challenges that require some sort of response. The nature of the action we choose will determine the nature of the outcome. Actions to our everyday challenges are divided into three energy types: **Positive action**, **Neutral action**, and **Negative action**. For those who seek to gain more control over their lives can learn these three factors. Let me further explain and define these three types of action that had an tremendous effect on my life.

"Positive action is a response that provides positive feedback to situations, circumstances, and challenges that will eventually lead to a positive outcome." (Reacting with a positive mental attitude) Usually when we face obstacles, we perceive them to be negative. In most cases, they usually are. However, when life places you in negative situations and you react with positive actions, the situation tends to iron out and you discover there was really nothing to worry about. If we can create a habit of performing positive actions with all our situations, we would live a much more positive life with more positive results no matter what we decide to get into (business, relationships, etc.)

"Neutral action is a response that is neither positive nor negative." Nothing is gained or lost from this type of action. Depending on the type of situation, circumstance, or

challenge that you go through, the outcome will remain unchanged. It's the equivalent of doing nothing at all. Choosing to do nothing is still a choice and therefore a form of action.

"Negative action is a response that provides negative feedback to situations, circumstances, and challenges that will eventually lead to a negative outcome". For example, you encounter a negative situation and you react with negative action. I can guarantee you that you will not like the final result. It goes to that saying, "an eye for an eye will leave the whole world blind". This is why revenge will always hurt both parties in some way, fashion, or form.

And the main reason why someone said that if you seek vengeance, dig two graves: one for you and one for the other person. When it comes down to handling problems at work, panicking and going into a frenzy (negative action) will only ensure that the problem gets worse.

My point is this: if we all embrace positivity as the centerpiece to our lives, we will reach our goals faster and live a productive lifestyle. Keep adding positives to your life and watch how people respond to you. Positive power is far more powerful than that of negative power. The more you generate, the more your life improves with every passing day.

We may have reached the end of this book, but your journey is far from over. Now go over this book again and begin to apply each principle to your life. Read a principle, apply the principle. This is how you initiate the *momentum*. No matter where you are in your career or business right now, you can always change it up and use what you have learned from the book to dramatically increase your annual income. Remember this always:

"You attract what you fear. Fear nothing, attract success."

BONUS SECTION

The Coach's Corner

"The Key to Building An Empire: The Power Behind The Mastermind"

When building anything, especially a profitable business, one won't be able to do it alone. A team is needed. Not just any team, a mastermind group. Now what is a "mastermind group"? When you break it down to its basic fundamental element, it's the gathering of the greatest minds. When I say "greatest minds", I am referring to people who are dedicated to achieving the same goal as you. With everyone within your mastermind working together as one, unstoppable force, the possibilities are endless.

Now the real question in today's world is: Why do so many people fail at building a real profitable empire? Too many people rely on the thought that "I can do this all by myself". Granted, there are some things in this world that nobody else can do but you. However, holding on to that thought when attempting to build a legacy for yourself will kill any chance of you succeeding in creating something special for the people you're trying to serve.

Take the creator of Facebook for example. Even though his mastermind wasn't that big, it was enough to build a platform that the entire world uses. Steve jobs is another example of the power that a mastermind group holds in creating a great product. Here are 3 tips that will help you get a good idea on what a mastermind is and how to put one together:

-Understand what "synergy" is. Synergy is the interaction of elements that when combined produce a total effect that is greater than the sum of the individual elements. In other words, this is the power that a mastermind group holds. Your individual acts may create great results. However, when you combine your efforts with others moving toward the same goal, the end result is 10x greater than what you would have produced by yourself.

-Find your "12" individuals. Within the Bible, it tells more of how Jesus put together his team than what he did on his own. There is great wisdom there and proof that we can accomplish greater things when we work together. Although, it doesn't have to be 12 people, it's a nice number to aim for when putting together your mastermind.

-Don't overload with dead weight. I highly recommend when putting together your team that you consider what their desire is. Having a lot of people in your group with different goals can create a chaotic and unorganized environment. If you must have a lot of people on your team, use the 12 method I mentioned before and ensure that everyone is on the SAME PAGE. This will maximize your results in the end.

-Seriously, get to know each other. A mastermind works a whole lot better when all the members are friends. Get to know your team. Find out what each person likes, their dislikes, and their dreams. Become a family in other words. This will increase the energy flow within your mastermind and will produce high quality ideas and concepts that will take each person's bank account straight to the moon.

It's not all about earning money. You can use these tips to build a mastermind for any major goal you may have. The sky is the limit. It's time to start building your team and create a legacy that will go on far after you're gone. Make every day count!

"Decisions: The Perspective You Give Them Determines The Outcome"

Is there such a thing as a "bad" decision? When you break it down to its simplest form, you realize that bad decisions are nothing more than decisions. In truth, there is no such thing as a bad decision or good decision. There are just decisions we make and how we feel about them after we made them. For example, just because we made a decision for ourselves and others perceive it as "bad" decision, doesn't make your decision a bad one. That feeling that others get is based off of their wants, needs, and desires of whatever you're deciding for or against. So many people beat themselves up over a decision they made based off of what other people perceive it as.

It's pointless to go on this way. If you feel as though the decision you made was the right one, nothing else truly matters. Often times, people make a decision to quit their job to pursue their dreams. Often times, other people will tell you that making that type of decision is too risky, therefore, deeming it a bad decision. Questions arise such as, "why would you leave the security of a "well paying" job to chase some dream that will never come true?" Now here is the amazing part. Once you achieve your dream and the level of income you had once strove for, your "bad" decision automatically becomes a great decision to those who doubted you before.

People will judge you no matter what you do. Who are we to judge your calls? Who are we to say that the decisions you make are the best or bad ones? The only time your decisions become bad is when you deem it so. The only time your decisions become a great learning experience, is when you deem it so. Do you see how this works now? You control

The Coach's Corner

100% of your feelings toward any decision you make. Make a decision today to stop allowing people to tell you if your decisions are sound. Make decisions based off of your intuitions and use the power behind to transform your life the way you want.

"Finding Your Inner Leader: Taking The Mantle Of Success"

If you're looking for a leader, you don't always have to look toward the front to find it. It starts in the back, the wash room, the lower levels of a company, and at the bottom of the tree of a network marketing business. It all begins with you. When it comes to going to the next level within your business, career, and life, one must take the mantle of the leader. Think of it this way, when you look around and see all those millionaires, multi-millionaires, and billionaires, where do you usually see them?

Surely you wouldn't find them following the crowd and doing what everyone else was doing. These are the individuals who decided to think differently than everyone else. They decided to lead their own lives to become financially free versus letting someone else lead it for them (which usually leads to nowhere).

Leaders are made when the necessity of change becomes greater than the acceptance of mediocrity. Most times, you will hear excuses like, "Leaders are born. I'm not a natural born leader, so it's ok to be a follower." This simply isn't true. Sometimes our very best leaders are those who once sat in the back of the class or the meek person who kept to themselves. I was once the quiet boy in school who kept to himself. However, my need for change became greater than my want for mediocrity. That's when I got angry at my circumstances and decided to change my way of thinking.

Can anyone do this? The answer is YES! Anybody who desires change can and will become a leader once they decide to take control of the outcome of circumstances that may be "hindering" them at the time. Now you will bump into opposition when deciding to move up the ranks and you will feel certain types of resistance from other people.

Here are a few things to remember when becoming a leader:

-Reaching a new level means experiencing a different set of challenges: It doesn't matter what level you're on, you'll face challenges and as you go up, these challenges tend to change along with your ascension. Embrace these challenges and do not fear failure. Failure is key to succeeding. Don't allow a temporary setback (failure) to stop you on your journey. Learn from failures and move on to the next step.

- When building something new, you will have to battle to protect it: You will bump into other people who have the "crab in a bucket" mindset and they will do everything in their power to try and stop you from rising. Typically the crowd you use to be with will do their best to keep you there. Keep moving forward even when they are "shooting" at you. Just because they are shooting at you doesn't mean they shot you. That will only happen when you allow them to.

The Coach's Corner

-Commitment without character is Hitler: Bishop T.D. Jakes said it best when he stated that, "when you have commitment without character, you get Hitler." Being committed to reaching a goal is one thing. But when you work people that may be a part of your team beyond their limits, you might as well be a dictator. Therefore, you become a BOSS. When you have a BOSS mindset, Big Opportunities Seem Small. Then you miss opportunities that can help you and your team reach your goal faster and better (because everyone would be happier).

-Step out on faith: Believe in yourself, keep moving forward one step at a time, and you will achieve the change you seek.

Lead your own life, control how much you earn per year, and how your life turns out. Followers are everywhere. However, leadership begins with you.

"Withdraw From Your IBA: Cashing In On Creativity"

For centuries, people have been searching for the source of ideas that can transform a person's life financially forever. Few people figured out what it took. It is the source of our creativity. It's where crazy ideas come from and how one's bank account jumps up several zeroes. Allow me to reveal to you a concept that will change your entire way of thinking when it comes to being the originator of great ideas.

If you want to increase what is in your real World Bank account, draw from your "IBA" (Infinite Bank Account). Rather than money being in this inner account, are ideas and concepts worth millions. All you have to do to withdraw from this account and cash in on those ideas is to act on them. Simple to do for the few who understands this basic concept. They are the people who other people are working for.

For many who understands this concept and choose to go for the "illusion of being safe" route, this may be a hard and rather difficult concept to grasp. However, the key to having a massive bank account is to have a very open mind. Those who find it hard to commit to this concept are the very same people who commit their time, money, and resources to build millions for other people.

People like Bill Gates used this very same concept when he created Microsoft. Mark Zuckerberg also withdraw from his IBA to create Facebook making him the youngest billionaire ever. We all have an IBA within our minds. The question is: How do you access this vault of gold?

-Find a quiet place to go to. No distractions. No TV, no computer, no radio. All you should have with you is a pen and paper to write down your ideas

-Close your eyes and reach back into the darkest regions of your mind.

-Think back to when you had an "ah ha" moment or when a crazy idea hit you.

-Think of things you see that can be done better if done differently, no matter how silly you think it is. Make sure it's something that you feel confident that you can accomplish if you set your mind to it. If you feel you can't, do it anyway and surprise yourself.

-Open your eyes and write down all the ideas and new concepts that you withdraw from your IBA.

In the most common case, this is critical thinking. However, looking at it from the perspective of withdrawing from an inner bank account will help many to overcome the thought of this being a hard task. Take some time to go over this article and make as many withdrawals as you wish. There is no limit to what you can accomplish and no limit to your abundant ideas.

"What Create Results: Expand The Mind For Desired Outcomes"

Whatever goes on within the confides of your mind will surely reflect on your outside actions. What does that mean? What you think about and how you think about them will determine the level of income you earn, the type of house you live in, the type of car you drive, the type of relationships you have, etc. Take a look at what you have right now. Everything that you have around you will tell you what type of thoughts you grant attention to.

This can make a real impact on your life. Since your most dominate thoughts will determine the type of actions you take which will determine the type of lifestyle you live, it would be best to expand your mind by learning all that you can. A person who only knows of working for wages cannot hope to attain the millionaire mark. But by learning and applying different and honorable ways to earn income, the chances of attaining such a mark increase. I know we all said it before, "we heard that before. It's nothing new". There is a reason why so many people still work for wages and a small amount earn giant amounts of income. Because one may have heard helpful information before, doesn't mean that one utilizes it.

It is not enough to just "know" about something. It's useless if you don't put it to practical use. Here is one secret to success: Listen from those who have gone to where you want to go (i.e. books, mentors, programs, seminars), apply those steps to your own venture, and leave nature no choice but to send success your way. This alone will entirely change the way you think.

Therefore, changing your actions and creating a different set of results you wouldn't have gotten if you didn't apply the one secret to success. This also works on other aspects other than money. The bottom line: Expand

The Coach's Corner

your mind in the direction you want to go,
exceed your limits, and create desired results.

The Coach's Corner

exceed your limits, and create desired results.

"Time Travel To Wealth: The Key To Building A Solid Plan"

So how do dreams come true? How does one man accomplish the impossible by going from being homeless to multi-billionaire? How does one single mother become a millionaire practically overnight? Most of these situations would seem quite outlandish to say the least. However, it has been done many times before. I am about to unveil to you the secret that can cause such "impossibilities" to become your current reality.

By envisioning yourself performing the steps necessary to achieve your goals and doing exactly what you envisioned, you can bring a dream right into reality. All it would take is the correct mindset, a little imagination, and the drive to get it done. The #1 mistake a lot of people make when trying to apply this proven technique into their business, schooling, career, or job, is that they only envision the end result.

This will not be enough to ensure your success. It's perfectly understandable to think of the end first. So many coaches have recommended that by using that technique, it will get you where you want to go. It's great that you know what you want, but it won't get you there just by knowing.

Often times, I would envision myself doing more pro bono, volunteering at more charity events, getting the right people supporting me, speaking to more businesses and individuals, and watching the fruits of my labor pay off. And by acting on what you envisioned, the results come close to what you saw as your end result if not the exact picture you drew for yourself. Life is truly simple to understand and master. However, the journey won't be as easy as I make it seem.

You will encounter your fair share of challenges, but keep in mind that they are just that....challenges. You will eventually overcome them. They are nothing more than temporary inconveniences. They are not stronger than your visions.

Whatever you may be into at this present time, whatever endeavor that you're a part of, this technique of critical thinking will yield the results you seek from it. Remember, only you can determine the final outcome of your life and the final outcome of your bank account.

"Circle of Value: Taking a Look Into Our Inner Circle"

As your circle diminishes, you will notice the value has drastically increased. By circle, I mean those who fancy themselves as your "friends". Throughout life, you will gain new friends and lose old ones. But are those new one's really there for you or there with their own secret agenda? This is where I apply that ever so old philosophy, "everything happens for a reason". Everything happens with an intent to teach.

Normally to test your new "friendships", life will throw some pretty serious situations your way that will show you who really supports you and who doesn't. Serious events in your life will reveal the most valuable people in your circle. This also applies to business as well. You must be careful of who you let into your inner circle. Not everybody has the best intent for you, so be weary.

Having the wrong types of people in your life can seriously poison your progress for overall growth. If anything, it will stunt it. Have you ever noticed that you attract people into your life based off of the type of lifestyle you live? If you're a clubber, then it's highly likely that your friends are clubbers too. If you're on a path to becoming a millionaire, then your friends will be those who are ambitious enough to join you on the journey.

If you ever wonder where you're in life right now, just look at the type of company you keep around you. Birds of a feather flock together. Your circle doesn't need to be huge. It just needs to be big enough to fit the most valuable people you have. Value will take you much further than sheer numbers will. Remember, this doesn't make you a harsh person when you cut some people out of your life (Those who are only there for you when it benefits them). This makes you wise. Think on this and grow.

"Power of the Master Tool: The Master Key To Forward Movement"

Our minds are key to changing our ever promising future. It's a powerful tool. You can use it to build yourself up or tear your abundant future down. Whatever you decide to use it for, it will work, in the exact way that you intend to use it. However, there are many of us who don't fully realize just how powerful our thoughts have on their current reality. I have always said that "my reality is completely different from the reality that you live in. It isn't until we become like-minded individuals that our reality may become one and the same."

The Coach's Corner

It's true. Whatever you perceive to be truth, will be truth. Your perceptions about situations and circumstances derive straight from your thoughts and will completely alter your reality. For example, where someone sees losing their job as horrible thing, someone else may see losing their job as a message that they were destined for greater opportunities and positions in life. This is the person who will live a wealthy lifestyle!

Where someone sees being dumped by a girlfriend or boyfriend as the end of the world, someone else may see a greater door being opened for them to meet someone better. There are only two indicators when dealing with perceptions: negative and positive. Negative perceptions will only lead down the path of destruction, whereas positive perceptions will lead to more opportunities and potential growth.

Here is a tip you can use to change things around for you right now. Take 10 minutes out of your day to sit and think about all the negative circumstances and situations that you can benefit from just by changing your perception on them. You will discover that by doing this exercise, that things that seemed too big to handle will look like manageable tasks that can be taken care of quickly. The extra benefit, you'll learn something from the experience.

This is the power of thought. This is the power of your mind. It is said that the mind is a terrible thing to waste. Although this may be true, I believe that the power of thought is a terrible thing to let wonder in the wrong direction. You have a great tool that can create anything that you desire out of life. Don't allow the events of life to dull your tool of creation. Allow life's great lessons to sharpen it only.

"What Lies Beyond The Gate: Unlocking Your Path To Success"

Quite often, I like to talk to random people I meet when I'm out and ask questions regarding to what they do for a living. It's no surprise that the majority of the people I talk to work at a low end jobs. Then I proceed to ask would they like to be rich? The majority said no. Directly after, they would continue by justifying why they don't attempt to achieve wealth. I often heard, "money isn't everything", "money is the root of all evil", and "money changes people". I would reply, so why work at all for money if you truly believe all these things?

They would give me the most perplexing look. I gather that the reason that most people react to my questions that way is because they believe that they can't become rich. They believe in the "luck factor". That one must be lucky to attain massive wealth. This isn't true at all. We all have what you would call, the "Success Gate". Behind this gate would lie all your dreams made into reality. The problem is that most people see the gate, but never use the one key that can open it because of fear of the unknown. They don't know what will happen once they opened it. The key I am referring to would be courage.

To obtain happiness, one would need to be free. And how do you obtain freedom? You must have courage. Acting in spite of your fear. This alone will open your gate to the path of success. If you have a dream that you want to materialize into reality, but are afraid of possibilities of failure, move forward anyway. Push yourself and be courageous. I heard once before by an old co-worker I used to know, "fortune favors the bold". Truer words have never been spoken by this man.

The Coach's Corner

Fortune does indeed favor the bold. This is what creates the illusion of "luck".

Those who are afraid of failure, but move forward anyway, are destined for greatness. It's ok to be afraid. It's not ok to let that stop you. Fear is nothing more than an illusion. You will find that out once you walk right through it and onto the path to make all your dreams come true.

"The Master Key To Wealth: Unlocking Life Changing Events"

We all hold the key to unlocking our own financial freedom. We usually can find it weaved within what we enjoy doing most. If what you enjoy doing helps other people in the process, you will find out very quickly that the gift that was given to us at birth (the power to choose our own outcome in life) will guide you to the riches that is rightfully yours. But what stops most of us from ever discovering that key and keeps us in the depths of struggle most of our lives?

Mainly, the biggest obstacle that stand in our way to finding the master key to unlocking endless potential is OURSELVES. However, there are contributing factors that may convince you that you have no talent, no gift, no way of ever escaping the "struggle". One of those factors lie in what other people tell you. You may have heard things like: "You have no talent", "You're useless", "Stick to your day job", "I had a friend who tried that and it didn't work", and "What makes you think you can do it?"

Here is the scary part. These things aren't said by people who you don't know, but by those who are close to you! Instead of empowering you, they choose to discourage you. To keep you "in the bucket". With all this shade, it's no wonder that a lot of people stay where they are right now. Simply because they can't see what they have lying deep inside of them. Great rule of thumb when dealing with this hurdle: Discouragement from others is the key indication that you're on the right track to wealth. You have something they don't and they want to make sure you don't see that you have it!

Another factor is the fear of other people rejecting you because you choose to use your innate gift. Not being accepted because you choose to do or become something or someone different. Well, here is the truth to dealing with this hurdle: People will judge you no matter what you do. If you choose to do nothing, people will call you a "coward", "bum", or just plain lazy. If you choose to use your key, people will call you crazy, stupid, insane, or a hopeless dreamer. So in the end, it really doesn't matter what you do. What does matter is that you enjoy what you do.

Ultimately, the decision to do what you love and live among the financial elite is up to YOU. So if you haven't yet, GET OUT OF YOUR OWN WAY AND DO WHAT YOU LOVE! FIND YOUR KEY!

"The Cycle of Wealth: Change Your Life by Changing The Lives of Others"

While on this journey of mine to change the fate of those who seek the results they want out of life, I have discovered a power that can grant anyone all the things they could ever possibly need in one lifetime. This concept of this power is so simple that anyone, from any circumstance can overcome obstacles and challenges standing in their way. Did you know that when it comes to obtaining wealth in this world, all you need is the right opportunity? Now here's the thing, most people believe that opportunity is a rare commodity that only happens a handful of times.

This is not true at all. I live by one simple concept when it comes to obtaining the right opportunity: Why wait for opportunity when I have to power to create it? We all do. We all have the ability and inner power to create our own opportunities in life. Allow me to further explain what I mean. To create opportunity would mean that you're whole and one with yourself. You know what you what, who you are, the power that you hold to control the outcome, and where you're going. Here is another secret when it comes to obtaining the right opportunity. You can become that very opportunity you seek to change your life.

Within this quote that came to me within a dream, you will find all that you need to become your own hero: "Become that opportunity that can change your own life by becoming the miracle that can change the lives of others." In other words, by adding value to other people's lives with your product or the service you render, you in turn will add value to your own life, business, and/or career.

I call this the "Cycle of Wealth". It's an unstoppable force that has been the catalyst to the small percentage of the wealthy's success. If you doubt what I say, you need not look very far. Just think of how Oprah Winfrey got to where she is today. Think of how Bill Gates, Mark Zuckerberg, Dr. Dre, and other millionaires and billionaires that you may know of got to where they are.

The answer is simple when it comes to becoming wealthy: Think and concentrate on how you can serve your fellow man. Become the miracle that people seek. Solve problems that others feel they cannot. Become the solution, not the problem. When you act on these motives, watch your income and life grow!

"The Rule of 10%: The Millionaire's Source of Innovative Power"

Did you know that at least 10% of your thoughts hold the key to you changing your entire life forever? Seriously, within that small percentage of thoughts lie an idea that can take your income into new and damn near impossible heights. I recently talked to a man who was in their late 40's who was sick and tired of working at a job he thought was only going to be temporary. It would have been except he admittedly stated that he had great ideas that he thought could have made him wealthy, but then thought that they were "stupid" and dismissed it entirely.

In other words, he turned to the 90% of negative thoughts designed to throw him off and crushed his chance, before he even got started. 9 times out of 10, the ideas that you may deem "stupid" are the ideas that could put you in the financial free bracket. Walt Disney built his entire empire off of the rejections of his board of directives. Once they objected to his ideas and said that it would never work, Walt got started on them immediately. Needless to say, but I'll say it anyway, he made millions off of those ideas.

The next time you have an idea that you feel may work, write it down in your personal journal (assuming you keep one) to come back to it later. You would be surprised at what you think of once you see it on paper. Then start acting on those ideas. Most of us pray for a massive change. And when God answers you in the form of a thought or idea, we tend to quickly shut it down because it's different! If you try to take the easy road and do what's already been done, you won't see any outstanding results. You must be different than what's already out there. You must have a better idea. A different idea!

The Coach's Corner

Remember this article as the "Rule of 10%". Write down all your "stupid" ideas (which is the Rule of 10%), act on them, and watch what happens. This could very well be the deal breaker that takes you from $5,000-$50,000 per year to $200,000-$1,000,000 per year. Embrace change before someone else acts on the same "stupid" idea you may have had.

"Self-Education: Raising Self Value, Generating Greater Income"

You are your greatest asset. You can generate as much income as you want if you increase your value to the world. Question: You would pay a person who can help you with nothing to do nothing? Or would you pay a person who can help add self-value and help you change how you live forever? This is why self-development is so important when it comes to increasing your income. It is the difference between earning $20,000/year to earning $2,000,000/year. So why don't that many people do it?

The Coach's Corner

95% of people in today's world in America look at self-development as a waste of time because a friend of a friend told them that it was.

Those same 95% are either thousands of dollars in debt for schooling fees, working for that 5% of people who did undertake the "self-development course", or started their own business and failing miserably because they have no clue why customers don't see them as a "valuable asset". It was Jim Rohn who said, "Education will earn you a living; Self education will earn you a fortune". Self-education is a part of self-development.

It's time to stop listening to those who are a part of the "walking dead"(Those who look like zombies because their jobs won't allow them to sleep very often). For those of you who are looking for information that will set you up for success, I will provide a link that will give you all the answers you seek shortly. My point is this: You determine how you live, where you live, and how abundantly you live.

You determine how much income you earn and whether or not your children will be taken care of in case you depart from this world in an untimely manner. It's you and it always has been. I hope this clears up the confusion a little for why there is such a big difference between "the haves" and "the have nots". It's time for you to follow up and focus on your #1 asset for growth. Remember, your income changes when you do. Good day. "Face your Goliath and achieve the "impossible".

"Everything You Do Matters: Change Your Future"

You're capable of so much more than you believe. You have a power to change your destiny and rewrite the very fabric of how you live your life. It's true that we all are headed to the grave one day. But how you live your live until then matters a great deal. Will you be struggling or will you live abundantly? These outcomes are determined by your most dominant thoughts. What you tell yourself every day matters. How you choose to spend your day matters. Will you be out changing people's lives or will you keep to yourself?

Will you prepare for your retirement today or will you only focus on the present? Each decision you make to these simple questions has a direct effect on your lifestyle now and how you will live it in the future. Be very mindful of how you use your time here on earth. You never know when your time here will expire. Live every day as though it was your last and do what makes you happy.

Tell that person you been crushing on how you feel about them. It doesn't matter what their reaction may be. As long as you said what you had to say. Live with courage, die with no regrets and leave nothing unsaid or done. Become a SUPERYOU and never stop growing. Your successful lifestyle is as close as you want it to be. Just claim it and it shall be yours!

"Face Your Giant and Take Hold of Your Destiny"

Everyone should know the epic tale of David vs. Goliath. One man going up against an "unstoppable" giant. Despite his size, David faced his giant foe with faith in himself and in God which vanquished all fears. By hurling a stone with a sling with all of his might, he hits the giant in the center of his forehead and defeated him. Which surprised David because he didn't realize it would be that easy. By overcoming this challenge, he seized his destiny to become king.

The lesson behind that story is simple but overlooked by many. There is no challenge too great to overcome with the power of faith and action. There's nothing that happens to you in your life that you cannot overcome. Many times we allow our situations, circumstances, or challenges to overtake us. Not fully realizing that our dreams and desires lie beyond those challenges staring you right in the face.

For those looking for financial freedom and the right to live life on your terms, this can prevent you from ever getting what you want. With faith, you can overcome any obstacle and seize your success, whatever that may be.

The only person in this world that can stop you is YOU. You're more powerful than you think. Go forward and face your giant. Have faith and believe that you will overcome the challenge when you go to battle with it and watch a "miracle" happen. That was more than just a story. It was literally giving you the key to success.

Knowing this now, ask yourself: Will I allow my "giant" to overcome me or will I run right through it and take what's rightfully mine? Believe in yourself. Believe in your power!

"Unleash Your Inner CEO: Making TREMENDOUS Decisions....and Profit From Them!"

Made decisions are life changing. The power behind them are astronomical and has the potential, which has been proven many times, to change the world. If Henry Ford hadn't made the decision to never quit and create the automobile, who knows what we would be using for transportation. This also goes for many famous inventors, scientist, doctors, etc.

The Coach's Corner

We all have the power to change situations, circumstances, and even the lifestyles of countless others. Knowing this can bring you wealth beyond your wildest dreams. How the do rich keep getting richer? By constantly making a decision to place themselves in a spot that will bring in more riches. Taking control of your life is crucial for your success. Success cannot be obtained with the indecisive mind and it certainly won't be given to you.

This plays a big role for those who are in leadership positions. Being able to effectively make a decision is very important. People won't follow you if you aren't able to make a decision whenever problems or challenges arise. There must be a figure head. You must lead the charge.

When it's all said and done, this is what you need to do for your life. The difference between those who accomplish everything that they set out to do and those who don't lies in the decision making power and faith behind that power, which each side has.

The Coach's Corner

There are those who don't know how to make a decision. In some cases, they never had to make one for themselves because someone else was always calling the shots. Here is a few tips that will aid you whenever you must come to a decision.

Before you begin, try some deep breathing. It helps clear your mind so that you're calmly figuring out the solution, instead of frantically worrying about outcomes.

List your options. At first sight, it may appear that there is only one course of action, but that is usually not true. Even if your situation seems limited, try to make a list of alternatives. Refrain from evaluating at this point; brainstorm and write down every idea that comes to mind, as crazy as it may seem. You can always cross it off the list later, but with those crazy ideas might come some creative solutions that you might not have considered otherwise.

Then ask other people for suggestions. Be terse and ask them what they might do in your situation. Sometimes strangers can offer the most creative ideas because they do not share your assumptions or biases.

The Coach's Corner

Weigh the possible outcomes. For every option, list every possible outcome and label it as positive or negative. One way to do this is to put a plus sign (+) next to a positive outcome and a minus sign (-) next to each negative outcome; especially positive or negative outcomes can get two signs instead of one. Some people find it helpful to make a decision tree, which lays out every possibility in visual format.

For every scenario, think about whether the best possible outcome is worth accepting the risk of the worst possible outcome. If the worst possible outcome is completely unacceptable to you, meaning that you could never forgive yourself if it happens, then you probably shouldn't make that decision.

Make note of the likelihood of each outcome. Give each one a percentage (e.g. there's an 80% chance of this happening, and a 20% chance of that happening). Make sure your estimates are based on experience or observation; otherwise, your fear or excitement might distort your perception of probability.

The Coach's Corner

Consider which option will encounter the most resistance and why. Significant difficulty in implementing a decision can sometimes outweigh the benefits of the outcome, depending on the situation. Other times, it's the most resisted decision that would make the biggest difference.

Consult your intuition. You must feel comfortable with the decision. On your list or tree, place markings next to those decisions that are backed up by your intuition.

Make a choice. This is, of course, the hardest step, but there will hopefully be a decision on your list that is backed up by both logic and intuition. It should have more plus signs than negative signs, and it should have your intuition's approval. If things don't match up clearly, though, ask for advice from people you trust. This can be a good tie-breaker.

By using these techniques, you may come to a decision that may make you rich. Money tends to be attracted by those who know how to make a decision.

"The Power Of Fear And How To Overcome It"

What I am about to share with you may irritate or anger some of you. But it's the truth when you really look at it. It's better to hear the ugly truth and grow than to hear a beautiful lie and suffer for it.

"Fear of Failure"

Poor people look as failure as something that should be avoided at all costs. Rich people look at it as something that can't be avoided, but should not be feared. Poor people see failure as a defeat or loss. Rich people see failure as a learning experience

L

and gain the wisdom that comes along with it.

Failure, often times, is seen as a taboo. Mainly because the consequences of failure is punishment. And to punish failure is to increase mediocrity. Isn't it amazing how changing your perspective on failure can change your financial situation as well? Within the journal, I've seen the many failures that my mentor had to endure. Yet, he wrote one simple line after each failure: To fail is to learn how to win. The light had turned on for me. To fail is to learn ways on how not to win.

This is what I call the "win" mindset. With this concept, it's hard to recognize failure. And hard to fear it as well. So when taking the leap, know that failure will come your way. There is simply no avoiding it. But don't fear it, for it is only a lesson to learn.

"Fear of Success"

There are many who fail to transcend to the next level of income because of the fear of actually getting what they want. Let's further break down this subject. One may fear the responsibility of success once it arrives. They are afraid of having to maintain that level success for long periods of time. You do have people out there who believe that nothing good can last for long.

This simply isn't a valid truth. There is nothing in the "rulebook to life" that states that living a successful and quite profitable life will only last for a short time. The proof is all around you. You have millionaire and billionaire families that has been generating massive amounts of income for generations and still rolling strong.

Another side to this is the thought of losing those who you hold dear because of your success. This coincides with the fear of judgment from friends and family. In some cases, people will stop talking to you because you have chosen to change the status quo. The truth of the matter is that people don't like to be outdone or outmatched.

You may experience these "loses" to some extent, but it's nothing to fret over. Not if you want to be wealthy. Remember, people come and go in life. Change is necessary for growth. So if you do see this happening, resist the urge to chase after them.

The Coach's Corner

People make choices in life. Allow this to be learning experience on their part. It is entirely possible to outgrow people. This is what it all comes down too: one cannot reach the pinnacle of riches and wealth as long as this fear stays strong within the mind.

"Fear of Change"

The one thing in the world that is constant is change. This evolution of life cannot be stopped. So why do so many people fear change? We assume that change is a bad thing. This fear is completely irrational and, quite frankly, not important enough to even be a factor in your life. Yet, this fear is powerful enough to stop progress cold, cause people to become stagnant, and prevents good, solid ideas that can change the world from being born.

To set the record straight, there really isn't such thing as good or bad change. It's just simply change. And depending on how you see that change determines what effect it has on your life. Change will make you a millionaire if you know how to ride the tides of it. Every change that happens forces one to grow and readjust to the said change. Many people who don't cope very well with change is doomed to live a life of poverty and constant struggle. There is no point in sugar coating this truth. You bought this book for the hard hitting facts.

If you're one of those people, it's time to change your whole perspective of change. See every shifting situation as a lesson that will make you rich. Life is filled with moments that will define who you are. Those defining moments are more than likely a pending transformation that you may have to undertake. This fear will yield no profit for you. So this is when we drop this burden and accept change for what it is. A lesson learned

www.ingramcontent.com/pod-product-compliance
Lightning Source LLC
Chambersburg PA
CBHW051447170526
45166CB00001B/142

* 9 7 8 1 5 1 9 2 8 1 0 3 6 *